Kudzu vines, Georgia, 2000. *Küstner*

MUSIC MAKERS

Pool hall, Middlesex, North Carolina, 1998 *Duffy*

music makers

PORTRAITS AND SONGS FROM THE ROOTS OF AMERICA

Edited by Timothy Duffy

d   HILL STREET PRESS   ATHENS, GEORGIA

A HILL STREET PRESS BOOK

Published in the United States of America by
Hill Street Press LLC
191 East Broad Street, Suite 209 | Athens, Georgia 30601-2848 USA | 706-613-7200
info@hillstreetpress.com | www.hillstreetpress.com

Requiem for a Snake Lady by Peter Cooper is reprinted with permission from the March/April 2000 issue of *No Depression*.

Interview of James Davis by Val Wilmer is reprinted with permission from the January/February 1979 issue of *Blues Unlimited*.

Interview of Guitar Gabriel by Timothy Duffy and edited by David Nelson is reprinted with permission from May/June 1992 issue of *Living Blues*.

Interview of Boogie McCain by David Nelson is reprinted with permission from the February 1994 issue of *Living Blues*.

Library of Congress Cataloging-in-Publication Data

Music makers : portraits and songs from the roots of America / edited by Timothy Duffy.
    p. cm.
  Includes discography.
  ISBN 1-58818-085-9
    1. Popular music—Southern States—History and criticism. 2. Folk music—Southern States—History and criticism. 3. Blues musicians. 4. African American musicians. I. Duffy, Timothy.
  ML3477.M83 2002
  781.64'092'273—dc21   2002024142

ISBN # 1-58818-085-9

10 9 8 7 6 5 4 3 2 1

First printing

Eugene Powell's house, Greenville, Mississippi, 1996 *Küstner*

"Blues will never die because it is a spirit. It is an uplift and the way you feel it, that is the way it is. And it brings a lot of joy to people. Music is made to make happiness, make you smile and forget your troubles. In the Good Book it says to make a joyful noise. It doesn't say what kind of noise, just as long as you make one. So that is about the size of it. That is what we are trying to do."

—GUITAR GABRIEL

Freedom Creek Festival, Old Memphis, Alabama, 2000 *Küstner*

CONTENTS

B. B. King and Eric Clapton, London, 1997 *Duffy*

FOREWORD by B. B. King

I was brought up on a farm in the Mississippi Delta, plowing fields behind a mule. My mother's first cousin, Bukka White, was a real-deal bluesman who cut records for the Victor and Vocalion labels. I idolized him and his fellow bluesmen Lonnie Johnson and Blind Lemon Jefferson. The blues is about feelings and their blues meant hope, excitement, and pure emotion. Those artists' guitars sang just like their voices.

So many bluesmen and blueswomen have given their hearts and souls to this music. Unfortunately many never rise from obscurity or have only a brief moment in the spotlight and thus face hard times when they can no longer perform.

I met the Music Maker Relief Foundation's Timothy Duffy while recording my album *Deuces Wild* in 1997. I learned of the mission of the group and how it was helping document and nourish the musical culture in which I was raised. I was delighted to know that the foundation had taken a unique approach by helping these artists with their daily needs so they could return to making music.

Tim gave me a number of CDs of Music Maker artists' work and when I played them later that night in my Los Angeles hotel room, it was like breathing the good country air from back home. The music invigorated me. The cover photos struck me, reminding me of the musicians I grew up around. I knew that when people found out about the foundation's work, they would be happy to help and I encouraged Tim to be steadfast in his work.

By collecting Mark Austin's, Axel Küstner's, and his own photographs in *Music Makers: Portraits and Songs from the Roots of America,* Tim has provided an important and authentic document of this little known but vibrant world. This selection from the MMRF archives takes me back to the farms, the drink houses, the front porches, the kitchen tables where I first heard this music and began making it myself. By documenting the faces and the deep, soulful eyes of the people who make the music I love, these photographers preserve a dimension of blues culture that could easily be lost forever. *Music Makers,* like the foundation from which it takes its name, preserves an American essence we can't afford to lose.

I cannot encourage people enough to learn more about MMRF and to listen to the music that they document and promote. The compilation of Music Maker artists enclosed in this book will make you want to cry and shout for joy as only the real blues can do!

PREFACE

MOST OF THE MUSICIANS PICTURED IN THIS BOOK are beneficiaries of the Music Maker Relief Foundation. A few are younger traditional artists who support our mission.

These photographs document performers of contemporary country, blues, jazz, R&B, and gospel traditions. My approach is to spend large periods of time searching out musicians of older styles of music and begin friendships with them. I am fortunate to share this style of documentary photography with Mark Austin, Kevin Hoppe, and Axel Küstner, all of whose work appears in *Music Makers*.

This selection of my own and these other roots music-loving photographers' work comes from our personal collections. The photos were taken over the last ten years or so at the MMRF headquarters and at homes and music venues throughout the South. When I first started to put this book together I had a pile of the essential five hundred photographs that I wanted to present. It became clear that I could not use them all or even think about the thousands of negatives yet unprinted in our cabinets. I decided on these images because they are the very best of the core group of recipient artists that we have worked with over the years.

I wrote most of the text accompanying the photographs, but Peter Cooper, Taj Mahal, David Nelson, Lightnin' Wells, Wesley Wilkes, and my wife Denise all have contributed to this effort.

Drink Small's guitar and autoharp, Columbia, South Carolina, 1999 *Duffy*

Introduction

"Hold fast to dreams, for if dreams die, life is a broken-winged bird that cannot fly."

—LANGSTON HUGHES

THE ROAD THAT LED TO THE FORMATION OF THE MUSIC MAKER RELIEF FOUNDATION has been a long one. The journey started in 1989 during my last semester of study for a master's degree in folklore at the University of North Carolina at Chapel Hill. I documented James "Guitar Slim" Stephens for the university's Southern Folklife Collection, one of the nation's best archival resources for the study of Southern musical and oral traditions. Slim was an old blues rounder. He had been everywhere in the U.S. and soon introduced me to a host of blues artists in Greensboro, North Carolina. I drove him to play at house parties and he patiently taught me the subtleties of his guitar style. We spent a great deal of time together at his home and around the city. Within a year, Slim was overcome with cancer. On his deathbed he urged me to seek out his friend Guitar Gabriel if I wanted to continue my education.

I asked a few people about Gabe but no one would take a white guy to east Winston. After graduation I began substitute teaching, as jobs in folklore are few and far between. I had just started when I awoke one morning with a premonition that I was going to meet Gabe.

The phone rang and it was a job offer at the middle school in east Winston. During homeroom my first day I asked my students about Gabe. One told me he had been burnt up in a house fire and another confirmed that he was dead, then a small girl came up and told me that Gabe was her neighbor and very much alive. She gave me directions to a drink house.

I went after school that day and told a fellow named Hawkeye at the house that Guitar

Slim had sent me to find Gabe. He took me to Piedmont Circle, a housing project built on an old fairgrounds. That's where Guitar Gabriel lived.

I got out of the car as Gabe was walking up to his porch. He took one look at me and said, "Where you been so long? I know where you want to go. I've been there before and I can take you there. I'm an old man and my time is not long. When I die I want you to promise to bury me with my guitar."

Gabe soon led me into his world of Winston drink houses. There are no establishments for working-class African-Americans to go downtown and socialize in a city like Winston-

Mississippi, 1998 *Küstner*

set free very late at night, far from my car.

Gabe was not in good health and his wife Dorothy, though much younger than he, was ravaged by alcoholism. In the midst of this very dark place Gabe was a truly bright light and a very intense, warm man. He had spent a lifetime on the road performing his blues as he hoboed from town to town. He was a real legend among his people.

On a wall of his living room there was a newspaper clipping from the seventies. It told how Judge Bill Freeman dismissed him from charges of shoplifting wine and bologna after Gabe sang and performed "Amazing Grace" on his

Salem. Drink houses are neighborhood places where one can buy a beer and people can get together. The proprietors loan patrons money when their checks run out or give them credit. Each house has its own unique appeal and Gabe was beloved at them all.

I became a close friend to Gabe and he took me under his wing. It was not that easy at first. Folks in the community thought I must be a narc. Initially, Gabe could not even get me through the door of most of the drink houses—the owner would just slam it in my face. The police thought I must be in the neighborhood to buy drugs and pulled me over on a regular basis. One night after dropping off Gabe I was stopped, ordered out of my car and handcuffed, then taken downtown and put in a holding cell. They never said what they were arresting me for, but released me after I passed a Breathalyzer test. I was

guitar in the Forsyth County courtroom. After I read the article aloud, Gabe remarked, "When that lady fainted, I knew I was free."

We became inseparable friends and business partners. We had a simple management contract: if I ever cheated Gabe, he could shoot me. During the next few years we played at clubs and festivals throughout the Southeast, traveled to Europe, and even performed at Carnegie Hall. When we were not performing, Guitar and I were looking up the many old performers that he knew.

I would pick up everyone on check day in my old van and take them to the grocery store, then to the post office to get money orders, then downtown to pay utility bills and back home again. Every two months we would pick up a bunch of these old entertainers and go stand in the welfare-office commodity line to collect their free cheese. I was completely immersed in a world not often seen by young, white guitar players.

Artists such as Macavine Hayes, Mr. Q, Willa Mae Buckner, and Captain Luke became my closest friends. Some had worked in show business their whole lives, some just on weekends while holding full-time day jobs. Every one of them had a great story and every story was different. In addition to their love of music, they shared the constant struggle to make ends meet.

Whether living on meager Social Security checks or, in Gabe's words, "singing songs of the times for nickels and dimes," there was never enough money, even for the basics. I became deeply disturbed by the difficult choices they had to make each month: food or medicine, rent or the car, heat or the telephone. I dedicated myself to finding a way to help these artists and the many others that I was beginning to meet.

I set up office in a storage shed in the backyard of my small, rented house at the back of a used-car lot just south of Winston-Salem. From this tin shack I booked gigs and desperately tried to find recording deals for Gabe and the other performers. I made recordings of these old, sometimes ailing, disabled, or blind performers so that their unique voices could be preserved for future generations to study and enjoy. I communicated to everyone with postcards because I couldn't afford long-distance phone bills. The recording offers I could scare up were pathetic, usually no more than a thousand dollars for delivery of a completed album master and artwork. The gigs I could set up

Georgia, 2000 *Duffy*

were often not much better. By 1993, I had figured out that the present-day blues scene had very little to offer my friends so I began to reach out to a few family friends for help.

I had lost my dad to leukemia in 1986; he was a great lover of music and a fast friend to many. I began to make a few calls to those who had offered to help me if I ever needed them. The first to respond was my dad's best friend from Louisville, Kentucky. He sent to our small house a tractor-trailer full of Ensure, a nutrition supplement drink, for Gabe and Willa. It was a tremendous gift and helped keep these artists in good health.

Then audio pioneer Mark Levinson returned a call. Mark was one of the few clients that my father, an attorney, had kept after he became ill. A few months before his death, my father had won a very significant case which essentially retained Mark's ability to work in the hi-fi industry. I told Mark what I was up to and he invited me to come visit him.

In December 1993, I visited his stereo showroom in New York. Mark was stunned as he listened to my humble field recordings. I then told him about the awful living conditions of these artists. He was moved to help.

It was Mark who envisioned the nonprofit and gave us the name Music Maker Relief Foundation. We worked without sleep for two weeks remastering field recordings and writing the liner notes for the eight-artist compilation compact disc of traditional North Carolina blues, *A Living Past*. Mark began using this album to demo his audio system and started asking colleagues and customers to contribute to the cause. The audiophile community was generous and by January 1994, I had seed money and a foundation to run.

First, we established our mission. In our increasingly homogenous, media-dominated culture, the natural venues for many Southern artists have evaporated. Without a place to perform, these musicians are without an audience and have no means of making a living through their art. Furthermore, the creative process itself is suppressed when the artist has no instrument and can't even afford a decent meal. Music Maker Relief Foundation was set up to help the true pioneers and forgotten heroes of Southern musical traditions gain recognition and meet their day-to-day needs.

Then as now, many such musicians were living in extreme poverty and needed food, shelter, medical care, and other assistance. Music Maker's aid and service programs were established to improve the quality of recipients' lives and to affirm to these artists that many value the gifts of music and inspiration they have delivered to the world. Our mission was, and continues to be, to give back to the living roots of American music.

With our nonprofit status, funding, and mission clearly defined, we set about our important work. Back in Winston-Salem, I bought shoes, groceries, and medicine for Guitar Gabriel. I was able to get prescription medicine and heating oil for Willa Mae Buckner and help several other artists with much-needed life essentials.

With New York as our platform to the world, there was soon a steady stream of interest and a small trickle of donations. In October 1995, Mark met Eric Clapton at a bistro in Manhattan and shared the foundation's story. Intrigued, Eric came to Mark's showroom a few weeks later and spent the afternoon listening to field recordings and talking about blues artists and their music.

This meeting was a springboard for Music Maker to get the word out. We started getting occasional national press and meeting celebrities interested in our cause, among them B. B. King. Donations slowly continued to grow and we started to clarify our mission further and even add new programs.

Since 1995 MMRF has developed several programs to address our beneficiaries' needs:

- LIFE MAINTENANCE—*Grants for necessities such as food, medical needs, housing, etc.*
- INSTRUMENT ACQUISITION—*Provides quality instruments and maintenance funds to recipient musicians.*
- TOUR SUPPORT—*Provides funding and services to musicians wishing to tour and record.*
- EMERGENCY RELIEF—*Substantial one-time grants to recipients in crisis (medical, fire, theft, etc.)*
- VISITING ARTIST PROGRAM—*Brings artists to our headquarters for professional development and assessment of their needs.*

When we meet a new artist, we discuss his or her needs and desires, in terms both of their musical career and standard of living. Music Maker makes many grants of cash or in-kind awards. The size and shape of relief varies with the individual's needs and our available resources.

Our Life Maintenance program has made grants for purchased groceries, prescription medication, heating oil, and other basics. This area is perhaps the most disheartening. The need is so great that our resources alone can't possibly pull folks out of poverty.

Music Maker programs are most effective for people who still desire a career in music. Initially many artists we contact do not even own a decent instrument. We have made substantial progress in rectifying this situation. MMRF has procured high-quality guitars for dozens of artists including Etta Baker, J. W. Warren, Carl Hodges, Guitar Gabriel, Drink Small, Jimmie Lee Williams, Precious Bryant, and Cootie Stark. Other instruments have been purchased for or made available to artists, as have instrument repair and maintenance funds.

Winston-Salem, North Carolina, 1999 *Küstner*

Robert Thomas's house, Society Hill, Alabama, 1996. D.B.

Our Tour Support program is extremely dynamic. It can provide travel escorts (road managers of sorts) and backup musicians to take artists to festival performances nationwide and abroad. We have provided escorts to Precious Bryant, Captain Luke, Willa Mae Buckner, Macavine Hayes, John Dee Holeman, John Lee Zeigler, Rufus McKenzie, Big Boy Henry, Cootie Stark, Mr. Q, Carl Hodges, Guitar Gabriel, Jack Owens, Cora Mae Bryant, Mr. Frank Edwards, Neal Pattman, Beverly "Guitar" Watkins, George Higgs, Eddie Tigner, Algia Mae Hinton, and many others. We help artists get passports, usually a terrific scavenger hunt, as most recipients don't have a valid birth certificate or driver's license. Or if they do, none of the information (name, birth date, place of birth, etc.) is consistent.

When we met Eugene Powell, of Greenville, Mississippi, he was eighty-eight. Like some other recipients, he only wished to make a few public appearances each year. In spite of this, Eugene maintained a public persona and Music Maker's tour support program was able to supplement his income by providing promotional T-shirts that he could sell to visitors to his home. We also provided T-shirts for Willa Mae Buckner, Mr. Q, and Guitar Gabriel. Gabe used to proclaim, "Buy one of these cassettes and T-shirts and you will see my picture on your chest, hear my music in your heart, and you will feel good about yourself in the morning!"

More importantly, our Tour Support program is the program that provides artists a stock of their own CDs. A recording not only generates income for them through sales, but also is essential in getting artists quality bookings. Most significantly, it gives the artist a voice to their community and the world.

What is most rewarding to volunteers, patrons, and us is the transformation that takes place when the musical gifts of an artist who has been isolated and inactive for many years are suddenly rekindled. Fingers that haven't touched a fret board in ages become once again limber and articulate. Songwriters who haven't composed in twenty years rediscover their voice and realize that they still have much to share. What seems to make the differ-

Perry, Georgia, 1999 *Duffy*

ence is not the amount of monetary assistance received, but that someone cares and is interested in their musical expression.

In early 1996, N2K records offered me a job as a producer for a series of releases featuring Music Maker artists. They also gave a very substantial royalty to the foundation. My wife Denise and I traveled extensively across the South with our mobile recording equipment, meeting more incredible musicians and I started to put records together.

By this time the elderly Guitar Gabriel had been in and out of hospitals and was living in a nursing home. Denise and I had moved to an old farmhouse in rural Pinnacle, North Carolina. I had a large library of field recordings and a small salary as a producer and I was still dedicated to keeping the foundation alive. I would visit Gabe nearly every day and tried to get him out when he was up to it. He loved to go out to Bell Brothers Restaurant and eat their sweet potato pie. In March of 1996, Guitar Gabriel, the inspiration for our mission, passed away.

Denise and I were making field trips to Virginia, South Carolina, Georgia, Alabama, and Mississippi to locate and visit more artists. All the time I had logged with Gabe and his friends made it easier to get into these communities. Still, when I first went to visit J. W. Warren I had to talk to him through his closed front door for a good half hour before he came out on the porch to talk some more.

One December afternoon I went to the mailbox to find an envelope addressed to MMRF. I drove up the driveway thinking it was another twenty-dollar donation. Sitting in my car on top of the hill, I opened the letter and was amazed to find a donation for one hundred thousand dollars. I jumped out of the car and screamed for joy. Then, I turned around to watch my car roll down the hill. I had left it in neutral.

This began a period of extreme growth for the foundation. Knowing the immense need among our recipients, Denise and I immediately began to increase grants, expand programs, and add new recipient artists. We were able to provide monthly checks to artists so that they could afford their prescription medicine, food, and rent. Pianos, guitars, harmonicas, and banjos

B. B. King and Eric Clapton, London, 1997 *Duffy*

were purchased for a number of artists. We enlisted the support of National and Epiphone Guitars to sell to us at cost, doubling the impact of our Instrument Acquisition program.

By the late nineties, invitations for MMRF artists to perform were coming in from Europe and we were able to provide airline tickets for an escort to make the trip possible and successful. One artist had a house fire and another lost his home in a flood. Through our Emergency Relief program, MMRF sent a new guitar, amplifier, and a check for a thousand dollars the very next day. We became a solid resource to our constituents.

We soon discovered that if MMRF invested around five thousand dollars a year in an artist's career, that artist would be able to produce double or triple that amount with the resulting gigs and CD sales. Our goal was to empower these folks to accomplish what they had longed to do for many years. What had begun as a handful were now dozens of artists who were benefiting from our programs. What's more, they had come to depend on Music Maker being there to help.

Within a year, the foundation's coffers were once again dwindling. Without a word of solicitation, another one-hundred-thousand-dollar check appeared from the same generous benefactor as before. It was unbelievable. This patron, who to this day requests anonymity, became our backbone and is the unsung hero of our organization.

In the spring of 1997, Cello Recordings purchased my contract from N2K. Looking for further support I traveled with B. B. King to Los Angeles, London, and New York while he recorded his Grammy Award-winning album *Deuces*

B. B. King (center) with the Rolling Stones, Los Angeles, 1997 *Duffy*

Keith Richards, B. B. King, Charlie Watts, Joe McGraff, two unidentified fans, John Landis, Dan Akroyd, Los Angeles, 1997 *Duffy*

Ron Wood and B. B. King (seated), Los Angeles, 1997 *Duffy*

Wild. B. introduced me to many well-known musicians he believed would be supportive of MMRF's cause, including the Rolling Stones, Van Morrison, David Gilmour, Jeff Beck, Joe Cocker, Dionne Warwick, D'Angelo, Dan Akroyd, Bonnie Raitt, and perhaps most fortuitously, Taj Mahal.

Taj was immediately smitten with Music Maker. To this day he is an active supporter of the foundation, sits on our board of directors, and is an artistic consultant on most of our records. He came down to Pinnacle and recorded with MMRF beneficiaries Cootie Stark, John Dee Holeman, Algia Mae Hinton, and Neal Pattman. These albums and others, nine in total, were released and nationally distributed in 1999. He remains in close contact with us, visiting MMRF at our new headquarters in Hillsborough, North Carolina, for a week at a time and recording with visiting artists despite his own nonstop touring schedule. MMRF is most fortunate to have this legend champion our cause.

Taj was instrumental in helping us organize the Winston Blues Revival tour, which took Music Maker artists to thirty-six cities in 1998 and 1999. It was a great joy to be able to meet so many music lovers across America. I can't express how empowering the experience of performing on first-class

(Left to right) Peter O'Hare; Kenny Smith, bass; Juicy with tambourine; Taylor Moore; Albert Moore, drums; Sammy Lee; Willie King at the microphone; Aaron Hodges; Freedom Creek Festival, Old Memphis, Alabama, 1998 *Duffy*

stages and receiving national press was for Cootie Stark, Neal Pattman, Beverly "Guitar" Watkins, and other Music Maker artists. This sponsorship and tour introduced the work of MMRF to the world by printing tens of millions of advertisements incorporating black-and-white photographs of Music Maker artists and information about the foundation, which appeared in one hundred ten top U.S. monthly magazines and one hundred twenty-five weeklies over the course of two years.

Since 2000 the foundation has grown. With the loss of corporate sponsorship and without the help of a major record label, we decided to take matters into our own hands. With the help of Fred Tamalonis, we instituted a bona fide development strategy for the future that would not depend on any outside corporate entities. In the spring of that year Georgia philanthropist Bill Lucado took our mission to heart and pledged a challenge gift of one hundred thousand dollars. Our donors generously responded and surpassed Bill's generous gift. We remain steadfast in our commitment to grow the Music Maker Relief Foundation.

The music of the artists we serve is of the highest caliber, as demonstrated by the intensity and beauty of their recordings. These artists represent something of tremendous importance to our American culture. If so much of our musical world is based on such traditions, we feel that it is our responsibility to seek out those destitute artists who still carry on the authentic musical traditions and develop means of expression and income for them. We must assist these artists to get where they want to go, for their own sake as well as to preserve and nurture this vital music.

Music Makers: Portraits and Songs from the Roots of America represents a new chapter in America's ongoing interaction with our traditional musical culture. This book introduces a new cast of artists to dispel the notion that the most real and rooted blues no longer exists. We have "turned on" countless fans to these men and women, revealing new icons for lovers of this music to treasure. Through the years, many younger musicians have apprenticed with these artists and have gone on to make successful careers. We have expanded the audience for these musicians, building cultural bridges for people throughout the world to learn and to understand and to dig what we are doing. Our work needs to continue to grow, as these musicians remain vibrant, expressive, and vital to our American experience.

(Left to right) Travis Hodge, Sputty Spann, and Shon Horn; Old Memphis, Alabama, 2000 *Küstner*

Beverly "Guitar" Watkins, Atlanta, 1999. *Duffy*

THE ARTISTS

Little Pink Anderson

Ever since that big crap game, I've been living off chicken and wine.

Born in 1954, **LITTLE PINK ANDERSON** of Spartanburg, South Carolina, began singing at medicine shows and carnivals with his legendary father Pink Anderson at the age of three. He still performs the highly entertaining old folk songs that his dad made famous, such as "Travelin' Man" and "Cook Good Salad."

HIS DADDY AUTOGRAPHED THE SIDEWALK, christening the wet cement at 583 Carpenter Street, and no one in Spartanburg gave a damn. His daddy died in poverty, unaware that he'd inspired luminaries such as Johnny Cash or that a British art rock band had combined his first name with that of another obscure bluesman (Floyd Council) and made it their own. His daddy sold bootleg whiskey, and he got a pretty penny for the hooch come Sundays. His daddy lay dead in the cemetery ground without a marker until some Yankee devotees named Roy Bookbinder (these days, it's Roy Book Binder) and Paul Geremia anted up about sixty dollars for a small piece of stone that reads PINK ANDERSON—RECORDING ARTIST.

Now here's the son, and he's singing his daddy's songs, in his daddy's medicine show style—vaudeville-meets-Hicksville ditties about greasy turnip greens and the god-forsaken Nasty Branch and West Henry Street and how you need five women, 'cause two might quit you and the other three might die.

Little Pink comes by this stuff honestly. His daddy taught him about guns and about money, and the lessons were readily learned. But he also taught him about the power of laughter and the glory and grace of song. He taught him how to play a guitar, and the first lesson learned was "St. James Infirmary." He taught Little Pink a version of "In the Jailhouse Now" that references Spartanburg's Broad Street jail, where Little Pink would later serve time.

"I used to think that the guitar was just good to get a few extra dollars and a woman," Little Pink says. "[Daddy] told me, 'One day, you gonna pick up that guitar and you gonna take it serious. That guitar will feed you when nothing else will.'"

So now Pink is a hero of the American roots music scene and Little Pink is a free and affable man, bent on preserving his daddy's legacy and on securing a page of his own in the grand story book of the blues. He has it to do over again.

His work is both subtle and mighty. It's beautiful and funny and heartbreaking and chilling. It's virtuosic and elemental. It's a piece of Pink that no one but the son could replicate, and it's a testament to Little Pink's own individual gifts. He's a bad ass, no matter where he came from, and if he ever puts his index finger into wet cement and scribbles *Little Pink Anderson*, everybody damn well better pay attention.

—PETER COOPER

In her garden,
Morganton, North Carolina, 1996 *Duffy*

Etta Baker

"Because she was a stunning beauty, Etta's husband refused to let her travel and perform away from home. She never stopped playing the music! This gracious grandmother was the source of a great deal of joy and surprise when I found that she still played guitar after I had heard her early recordings in the sixties. One of the signature chords of my guitar vocabulary comes from her version of 'Railroad Bill.' This was the first guitar-picking style that I ever learned."

—TAJ MAHAL

ETTA BAKER of Morganton, North Carolina, was born in 1913 and has been playing guitar since the age of four. She is the premier woman Piedmont blues guitarist. Her only contemporary was the late Elizabeth Cotton of Carrboro, North Carolina. Etta maintains a beautiful garden—an Eden of flowers, herbs, shrubs, healing plants, and fruit trees. She works in her yard every morning, coming inside only for lunch. Etta is constantly working on new arrangements as she plays the guitar every day.

Etta Baker's kitchen,
Morganton, North Carolina, 1998 *Duffy*

Elvershausen, Germany, 1995 *Küstner*

Robert "Wolfman" Belfour

I could never get away from the guitar. It was something that I could do, and then I could lay it down, set it back in the corner, and I had to go back and get it. Something always would bug me to play. I'd go to sleep with it in my lap.

Axel Küstner and I were returning home from a long fruitless trip to Greasy Corner, Arkansas, to locate and record "The Flying Black Eagle," a little-known harp player who we later found out died only a few weeks after our attempts to find him, and we drove through Memphis. Axel lead me to **ROBERT "WOLFMAN" BELFOUR**'s door. On a hot summer day this man performed in the rare guitar style of the North Mississippi hills. He told us that he had been born in 1940 in Holly Springs, Mississippi, and back there in the country at a house party, he might play just one song for two hours at a time as the people danced.

With National guitar, 1997 *Austin*

Sammy Blue

SAMMY BLUE first heard the blues as a young child at family picnics where blues legend Buddy Moss often performed. Sammy lives outside Atlanta and has created his own unique blend of urban and country blues.

"Sammy Blue of Atlanta is one of the best-kept secrets in roots music. I have been watching him develop over the last thirty years. He has an awesome delivery and presence. What is really very exciting is his writing and arranging style and the instruments that he brings together. It will keep you listening and coming back for more."

—TAJ MAHAL

Pinnacle, North Carolina, 1999 *Duffy*

Essie Mae Brooks

ESSIE MAE BROOKS was born in Houston County, Georgia, in 1930. Her father was a great drummer in the nearly forgotten African-American tradition called drumbeat. He would play the drum every weekend and people would gather and dance all night long. Her grandfather was a harmonica player and Essie started singing to accompany him. She began singing and writing gospel songs as a girl and has never stopped.

"Rain in Your Life"

This old life of mine, I sure had my ups and downs.
I've been up and I've been down,
I've been pushed and shoved around,
I've been picked at and picked on, but that's alright.
You got to have rain in your life to appreciate the sunshine.

When I lost my mother, you know it was sure enough rain,
When I lost my father, you know it was sure enough rain,
When I lost my sister, you know that was more rain.
You got to have rain in your life to appreciate the sunshine.

Lord, when trouble get all around.
That ain't nothing but rain.
When trouble get all in the way, that is nothing but rain.
When trouble get all in the home, that is nothing but more
    rain.
You got to have rain in your life to appreciate the sunshine.

If you never had no rain in your life, then you don't know what
    I'm singing about.
You got to have rain in your life to appreciate the sunshine.

Charlotte, North Carolina, 1998 *Duffy*

Cora Mae Bryant

from "McTell, Moss, and Weaver"

McTell, Moss, and Weaver, they was real good friends,
They stuck to one another until the end.
They gone and left me behind, sometimes I feel like crying.
I miss McTell, I miss you Moss, and I miss you Curley Weaver,
from being around here.

CORA MAE BRYANT is the daughter of Georgia guitar legend Curley Weaver. Curley would perform from one house party to the next, often meeting up with his friends Blind Willie McTell and Buddy Moss. Cora Mae was there, taking it all in, singing along, sitting on the knees of the men that created this music.

"When we was out partying, they loved to hear all Curley's songs but two they especially loved was 'Ticket Agent' and 'Tricks Ain't Working No More,'" Cora Mae says. "You could really hear their feet stomping. Daddy and I used to sing 'Wee-Wee Hours' together, it was really pretty."

Cora Mae Bryant is a blues scholar and her house in Oxford, Georgia, is a veritable blues museum. She can tell you everything you need to know of the old blues.

With Lucas Duffy, Warm Springs, Georgia, 1999 *Duffy*

Precious Bryant

I will always be playing the blues. As long as I live. The blues tells the truth. Sometimes it be sad, sometimes it be happy—it works all kind of ways.

PRECIOUS BRYANT has a sparkle of light that shines deep into the heavens when she sings and plays her guitar. She was born in rural Talbot County, Georgia, in 1942 into a family of traditional musicians that included many blues players and gospel singers. She is a talented, haunting, woman who writes from real life and is one of only a handful of living traditional blueswomen.

With Pepe and Siam, Winston-Salem, North Carolina, 1998 *Austin*

Willa Mae Buckner

In her days as a touring performer, **WILLA MAE BUCKNER** was known as the Wild Enchantress, Princess Ejo, the World's Only Black Gypsy, and, most often, the Snake Lady. She had been a tent-show performer capable of enthralling crowds in just about any form imaginable—as a blues singer, burlesque stripper, contortionist, and fire swallower. Born in Augusta, Georgia, in 1922, she was an articulate, self-educated, and fiercely independent woman who blazed her own trail from the day she ran away from home and joined an all-black tent show at the age of twelve. Her frank wit and exotic past always set the tone when she sang her risqué songs.

Willa was among the first recipients of aid from the Music Maker Relief Foundation's programs. MMRF was able to provide the money she needed to buy the expensive medicine for her chronic gout which she had often done without. The foundation transported her to numerous gigs including a performance at Carnegie Hall for which she received a standing ovation. MMRF bought her heating oil in the winter and placed her in a nursing home when she broke her hip. We provided comfort in her final days and sadly arranged her funeral in 2000.

Requiem for the Snake Lady
"At Least I Saw Something"

IN WINSTON-SALEM, NORTH CAROLINA, where more than a few people own decorative license plates reading "Tobacco Pays My Bills," take the Waughtown Street exit and then maneuver toward the Alverado Joyeria. That's a jewelry store, and that's where you turn on your way to the Johnson-Howard-Robinson Home of Memory, where they came on a warm January afternoon in 2000 to pay final respects to Willa Mae Buckner, the Snake Lady.

Reverend Sam Hickerson, though he'd never met Buckner, officiated at the funeral service. He wondered out loud in the eulogy what it was about this lady that could have brought such a diverse group of mourners together. He didn't know the answer lay not only in the kindness of her sweet old soul but also in her bawdy songs, her carnival background, and her great love of the devil's own metaphor.

"She was a good friend," Tattoo Joe said after the service. "She had her snake show back when I had my freak show, and we traveled around together. First time I saw her show, I looked at those snakes and said, 'They'd make nice boots.' She heard me and cussed me out. She cussed better than a sailor."

But Willa—Willa who spoke seven languages, loved Jesus, and prayed often, messed with an old black hoodoo pot, stripped at midnight rambles in the 1940s, started Christmas shopping in the summer, swallowed swords, and sang "Let Me Play With Your Yo-Yo" at Carnegie Hall—Willa Mae Buckner is gone. In her life she was shot, slurred, hassled, and harassed. She never left home without lipstick, high heels, and a knife, and she knew how to use all of those to best advantage.

"She was a combination of Granny on *The Beverly Hillbillies* and some seriously crazy black burlesque queen from back in the day," said blues legend Taj Mahal. "Willa Mae was as real as it's going to get in this century, or in the next."

New York, circa 1950
photographer unknown, Duffy collection

Winston-Salem, North Carolina, circa 1959
photographer unknown, Duffy collection

dancing. "They liked my daddy's home brew, but they favored my mama's moonshine," Buckner recalled.

Her mother's death was followed by father Freddie Morgan's hasty remarriage. Buckner said she was treated unfairly by her stepmother, left home at twelve, and spent a year at her uncle's house in Winston-Salem. One night when Willa was fourteen, she attended a minstrel show belonging to either Jimmy Simpson or Jimmy Samson (sources offer varying names). By the next morning she was dancing in the chorus line. She eventually moved into a more prominent role, performing risqué blues songs for the men who gathered:

As to what Willa Mae Buckner meant to American music in the twentieth century, it's hard to say. Her libidinous signature songs, "Peter Rumpkin" and the aforementioned yo-yo treatise, are not particularly well known, and Buckner's music is available only on two Music Maker compilations.

Buckner was a genuine trailblazer though, a true attraction on the poorly-documented carnival and medicine show circuit. Like long-dead medicine show vets Pink Anderson and Peg Leg Sam, Buckner borrowed liberally from vaudeville, knowing full well that the strange, sexy, or hilarious was more likely to draw paying customers than the heartfelt and forlorn.

Buckner said she had a happy time of it until her mother died when Willa was eleven. Before that, her home was something of a neighborhood hang-out and Buckner remembered fish fries at the house, complete with loud music and

Brother Jim, what's we gonna have for supper?
The heck with a man who's got a wife
And don't know how to. . . .
Fumble dumble, all night long,
Whiskey's in this glass.
Anybody here don't like this song
They can just. . . .
Kiss me once, kiss me twice
It's been a long, long time.

Buckner accompanied herself on piano, which she said she learned at age twenty-one. She taught herself to play guitar midway through her next decade, and would gig at clubs or minstrel shows.

But she didn't just sing and play at the midnight ramble posing shows: when the carnival would close its doors to children, she'd stand naked on a curtained stage and the drape would be slowly parted. There she would remain motionless for a couple of minutes, until the curtain closed again.

"You couldn't move a muscle," Buckner explained to friend and blues chronicler Gaile Welker. "It was against the law to move while you were doing that, and the law would watch you on that stuff, too! They could close down a show if you messed up."

Buckner worked all sorts of carnival shows in the early years of her career. "I worked the nail bed," she told Welker. "I ate fire. I also did the bronze dance: that's where you go all over the body with mineral oil and you put that gold paint on. You did contortions when you were in that stuff, and if you weren't careful you'd fall flat on your rear or your belly one."

In 1946, Buckner decided to get off the road and settle in Spanish Harlem. She sewed, worked at restaurants and in other people's homes, and she studied foreign languages at night school. She also took lessons in tap and gypsy-style belly dancing and played with a calypso band in small clubs.

She was forty-two when she began making plans to get back on the road. The 1964 World Fair's was held at Flushing Meadows in Queens, and among the featured performers was a Moroccan snake handler. She thought to herself, "If this man can come to my country and make money showing snakes, I'll bet I can, too."

Snake pit, circa 1965
photographer unknown, Duffy collection

And, as it turned out, she could. After building a healthy collection of twenty-eight snakes, she went to Philadelphia, bought a truck and a tent, and joined up with a traveling sideshow. She began billing herself as Princess Ejo, the Wild Enchantress, or the World's Only Black Gypsy, and her snake shows were popular facets of various carnivals.

"She would stand in the pit and talk to the people, tell them about the snakes," said Tattoo Joe. Joe, who is white, said his friendship with Willa was a natural, despite the segregation-era South's discouragement of such relations. "Race was never a problem with carnival people," he said. "Back then, carnival people stuck together."

Buckner said that when she was on the road she would let all those snakes out on the side of the highway and go walking through a field with them. When she wanted to get back on the road, she'd hide behind some bushes. The snakes would get scared and go back to the truck.

While Buckner was still not afraid to show some skin, her 1960s snake shows were mostly educational. She'd lecture about the animals while snakes slithered around in a pit or draped themselves over her body.

In 1973, Buckner's truck broke down and she left sideshow life to settle near her family in Winston-Salem. She took a job driving a city bus and even took care to curb some of the behaviors she'd acquired along the way.

She kept the snakes, though, and remained a well-known figure in East Winston-Salem, where people gathered for bootleg booze at drink houses like Ezelle's.

"The first I heard of her I was at Ezelle's with Guitar Gabriel in 1989," Timothy Duffy said. "This old lady came by, offered to sell Gabe an old Epiphone guitar and walked out. A couple of days later I was at the same place and she got up on a table and started singing these outrageous songs."

Thus began Buckner's third round in the spotlight. In January 1994, Music Maker Foundation began spreading the word about Buckner and other forgotten heroes of the blues, including Winston-Salem basso-profundo Captain Luke, gutbucket howler Macavine Hayes, and the mysterious Mr. Q. That same year she went back to New York, this time to play Carnegie Hall as part of a show called Circus Blues, sharing the stage with Guitar Gabriel, old carnival friend Diamond Teeth Mary, Smith McClain, and others.

"She loved to communicate with the crowd," said Winston-Salem writer John Creech. "She probably developed that ability from the hoochie shows of her past. She had gorgeous eyes, and they looked even bigger behind her glasses, and she had a face that was hard not to stare at for its warmth and beauty."

Buckner played numerous Music Maker package shows, some underwritten by a major tobacco company and presented as the Winston Blues Revival. Taj Mahal headlined some of those performances, including one at Charlotte's Neighborhood Theater in Winston-Salem in February, 1999.

"I would like to do this song as part of a striptease," Buckner said that night as Taj sang from the stage about how big-legged women were coming back in style. "I think it would be appropriate."

Backstage, Buckner looked a visitor up and down. "Have you seen my baby?" she asked, and pulled a photograph of a yellow python from her purse. Conversation then turned to carnival days. Buckner remembered

Winston-Salem, North Carolina, 1973
photographer unknown, Duffy collection

Lobster Boy, who used to travel the circuit. "He had hands just like a lobster, and he got married and his daughter had the hands of a lobster, too," she said. "We have so much to be thankful for."

By the summer of 1999, Buckner's mind and body began to shut down. She made it through the holidays, dying early in the morning on January 8.

Her death was cause for remembrance. Taj noted her skill as a businesswoman: "I don't think there's any era that could have repressed her," he said.

Creech recalled her laughter, and her skill as a put-down artist. He'd call out to her during a performance, yelling, "I'd like to play with your yo-yo," and she'd put a hand on her hip, point at him and say, "Boy, you got to be a man to be with this lady."

At the Home of Memory, they dressed Buckner up in a pretty blue outfit and put a wig on her head. She didn't look like a tough old carnie. Duffy and former LaFace Records session man John Ferguson played "Do You Know What It Means to Have a Friend?" before the service, and many in the congregation sang through tears. Duffy played Buckner's old Epiphone guitar.

"We are graveyard sons and daughters passing through an unfriendly world," Rev. Hickerson reminded the thirty-or-so assembled at what the Home of Memory program called Buckner's "Homegoing Celebration."

The world may be unfriendly, but Willa Mae Buckner was not. She was a woman who would sing for laughs when she couldn't sing for money, who worried over the comfort of snakes, thanked God that she didn't have lobster hands, and empathized with the carnival man who did.

"I didn't learn anything," she said after that show at the Neighborhood Theater, "but at least I saw something."

—PETER COOPER

Memorial to Willa Mae Buckner, Music Maker Relief Foundation offices, Pinnacle, North Carolina, 2000 *Austin*

Pinnacle, North Carolina, 1998 *Duffy*

Howard Colbert

I grew up around this music up here in the mountains, we got the blues up here too. It is just something inside of me that has to come out.

HOWARD COLBERT was born in 1950 up in the mountains in the western part of North Carolina in the town of Lenoir. He heard about MMRF's work and drove down one day to our then-headquarters in Pinnacle and spent a day with us sharing his repertoire of delicate traditional North Carolina songs.

"There has never been a day without picking on a guitar," Howard said. "I was twelve when I first got started. An older man name Leonard Wheatherspoon taught me the low-down blues. My Uncle Bill played the guitar and my dad played the banjo. In fact my father's dad and mom used to play as well. The first time I got a hand-clapping was at my eighth-grade prom. I got over my fear then of playing in front of crowds. Then later on down the line I went to New York and played in Billy Bland's group. He had the hit song 'Let the Little Girl Dance' [in 1960]."

"I stayed up in New York about two years and then I came home when my parents got sick," Howard continued. "To me, once you learn the blues you never want to leave it. There is something about the blues that will never die. It's been here."

Clarksdale, Mississippi, 2001 *Duffy*

Joe Lee Cole

I quit smokin' and drinkin' beer and wine and gamblin' and getting on my knees and shooting dice way back in the fifties. I'm way up in my eighties and I still feel like a man, right now.

I feel better now than I ever have, I got no complaints. Most of the people from around here have been dead. You can do too much of anything. One day I was walking down the road and I reached up in my mouth and threw that cigarette away.

JOE LEE COLE was born June 17, 1921, in Alabama but moved to Mississippi with his father at a young age. Cole moved to a former plantation—just south of Clarksdale and east of Bobo—in the early 1950s. Now in his eighties, Cole is the last tenant farmer left there.

IT's ONLY A SHORT TRIP FROM CLARKSDALE, MISSISSIPPI, to where Joe Lee Cole lives—just a few miles—but it was a good while before my friend and I actually found "the third beat-up shack on the left after the bridge and the derelict church" (Joe's directions). This is not a place where people live anymore. From what Joe told us, there had been more than fifty families living and working the area and, what's more, there had been a lot of music.

Since his wife and kids left him and moved up to Nashville, Joe lives alone, with a meager pension (he's a veteran) and eating mainly tinned soup and canned corn. He doesn't see many people.

You sense that it was mutual intolerance that led to the family's split, but Joe wouldn't have you believe that. As he told us, his wife suffered from "mentalations" which made her unbearable, and the kids always sided with her—who knows? Despite his laid-back manner and charming smile, you get the impression that Joe was not always easy either. Stories of him "fooling about, getting high and drinkin' too much" after an all-night jam-session in "them juke joints" and then "having to lie low for a while," recreate the atmosphere of the early decades of the twentieth century and the high period of local blues so vividly that it seems almost as though he is describing a film rather than first-hand experience. But he was a musician in the in the thirties and forties and—judge him as you wish—he lived that life.

I couldn't have imagined someone who embodied the blues as much as Joe Cole: of course there was the charm, the wily world-wise shrug, the wealth of experience, and the sheer authenticity of this life, but all of this is just cliché and nostalgia when one sees Joe's reality: it's lonely, it's squalid, and out there by the cotton fields one feels he's been forgotten in another era, left behind as a reminder of where the blues *really* came from.

But he accepts his lot with his trademark shrug, and is glad to have company for a while. The complete absence of self-consciousness is perhaps what is most surprising in Joe, and strangely the only time he ever manifests the slightest unease is when fumbling with the steel strings on his new guitar and struggling to work out a song he once sang long ago when there were people still around to hear. The song, when it finally crept out from between the strings and over Joe's softly rasping voice, was "Feather Bed," a song about the benefits of home and the numerous dangers of the outside world. It was one of the most beautiful songs I have heard.

Joe Cole *is* the blues in as much as he represents where the blues came from (both geographically and temperamentally), as well as the way in which certain communities, having been milked for all they were worth, have been forgotten. The poverty and abandon from which the blues first emerged still exists, just a few miles away from where busloads of blues aficionados and music journalists gather every few months for shin-digs, souvenir shopping, and high-brow chatter about chord structures.

It's true that one of the many appealing things about the blues is the nostalgia associated with its humble and difficult beginnings, yet to many blues artists the hardship of those beginnings has still not been overcome. While some of us are out buying our Robert Johnson CDs, people like Joe are living without electricity, with little food and little warmth, and often, perhaps most strikingly, without even the instruments which link them to the tradition they helped to create.

—TOBIAS MUNTHE

Clarksdale, Mississippi, 2001 *Duffy*

With Turi and Tobias Munthe,
Clarksdale, Mississippi, 2001 *Duffy*

With Fender, Freedom Creek Blues and Gospel Festival, Old Memphis, Alabama, 1999 *Küstner*

"Birmingham" George Washington Connor

"BIRMINGHAM" GEORGE WASHINGTON CONNOR moved from Pickens County, Alabama, to Chicago and stayed there close to thirty years operating his own blues club, The Place. In the eighties he moved to Memphis for five years before settling in Alabama where he opened another music hall. Unfortunately a few people got killed in it and the joint had to close down. George can be heard every year at the Freedom Creek Blues and Gospel Festival, in Pickens County, Alabama.

I used to live in Chicago for many years. Every summer my group would travel down South to Alabama and Mississippi and play at these juke joints. We would really bring a show and the people would come out, man, when they heard I was back in town.

Society Hill, Alabama, 1996 *Duffy*

George Daniels

GEORGE DANIELS still lives not far from where he was born in Macon County, Alabama, on April 27, 1929. He can really sing the blues and is a deep blues guitar and harp player. George treasures and nurtures the old ways in which he was raised. He still makes his own molasses and can distill a world-class rye whiskey.

George reflected on his lifetime of playing the blues: "I learned to play from my daddy. He gave me a guitar and I began to play when I was seven years old. The first song I learned was "Rabbit on the Log." I started blowing the harp for school marches. We had about four-piece marching band playing the harps. We were just little kids. We marched and blew for school events and such. I got into the blues when I was twenty-one years old. I got some of those records and I started playing behind them.

"My daddy was a farmer, I farmed a little while but I didn't like it, the money was too slow working on the farm. I went into cutting and hauling pulpwood, then I went into a mechanic shop.

"Back then they would have those old-time frolics and we played every weekend. That is when it was a dime a set. They would pay the musicians a dime for every round of the cakewalk.

"I played in the juke joints, it was alright—I still play in the jukes today. I'm an old man now and music is all about that I can do."

from "Coffee Blues"

Mama got mad at Papa
'cause he didn't bring no coffee home;
She went to Hurtsboro
and went to livin' with old Dave Stone.

Perry, Georgia, 1996 *Duffy*

James Davis

Middle Georgia remains a vast untapped area of undocumented musical traditions. **JAMES DAVIS** is from Perry, Georgia. His music stems from fife and drum music, which is among the oldest African-American musical traditions. His father played the drum and his uncle blew the fife. This music is simply called drumbeat. When I first met James in 1996, I saw simple flyers that promised "Drumbeat at the Turning Point." The Turning Point is the club where James played every Saturday night for many years. James played the old melodies of the fife with his electric slide guitar while his partner performed the old rhythms on a trap set.

"*The people around here call it the old country drumbeat. They like that old country-style playing. A lot of them say they'd rather hear my playing than hear them piccolos. I don't know what the drum do to people but look like peoples just enjoy drums. Somehow the drum just draws peoples—it always did an I reckon it always will. . . . Just 'bout all the records now that come out, you got some drums in there, it's coming from the spirit.*

"*I believe they sang blues before they sang spirituals, 'cause most times somebody strikes a blues, they can't even play a church song. Put it this way—the Good Book tell you if you're going to be a devil, be a devil. You can't serve two Gods at one time, so that leaves a gap. You either got to serve God or serve the Devil. I know who I be serving, it be the Devil-God. The Devil we say. But I look at it on the other hand and see there be a time for all things, a time to pray, a time to sing, a time to do anything we want to do. He only asks you for one day, we got six days to do what we want to do. I don't play none on Sunday, not no blues.*

"*You know, a lot of the spirituals got the blues in it. Some songs, the guitar player be playing the blues right along in that spiritual. The blues bad? Not for me, because what you like, you like. People say that, but that be a lot of them been too old for anything else! When he say that, he done everything he could do!*"

—AS TOLD BY JAMES DAVIS TO VAL WILMER AND FIRST PUBLISHED IN *BLUES UNLIMITED*, JANUARY/FEBRUARY 1979

Macon, Mississippi, 1998 *Duffy*

Albert Duck

My brothers and a couple neighbors and I used to have a string band. We played at picnics and there was many a day we did not have to go to the fields and work because we would be entertaining at the plantation houses for the big farmers. We played songs like "Alabama Jubilee," "Sugar Babe"—you know, popular tunes of the day.

ALBERT DUCK (1908–2000) was born in Prairie Point, Mississippi. He played string band music with his brothers in jukes around Macon, Shurlock, and Columbus, Mississippi. Alabama bluesman Willie King took me to his home in 1997 and they both sang "Sugar Babe," a tune which blues scholar Paul Oliver considers one of the oldest and most popular blues songs ever.

In front of portraits by Drew Galloway, Northside Tavern, Atlanta, 1998 *Duffy*

Danny "Mudcat" Dudeck

Born on the banks of the Mississippi and raised in Georgia, **DANNY "MUDCAT" DUDECK** dropped out of acting school in New York to pursue a blues major on the streets. Eventually he graduated to Atlanta where he converted the city's Northside Tavern into his personal school of music. His tutelage continues under Cootie Stark, Frank Edwards, Eddie Tigner, and Cora Mae Bryant. A world-class slide guitarist with a voice so rich it feels fattening, Mudcat's education is something you can feel right to your bones.

from "Rattlesnake"

I'm a rattlesnake curled up around your leg.
If you dig my sweet potatoes, don't make me beg.

I'm a jack rabbit, nibbling around your bush.
If you want my loving, give me a push.

I'm a bumble bee, buzzing around your hive.
If you dig my stinger, don't hand me that jive.

I'm a bullfrog, leaping around your pond.
It's your loving, I want to get on.

Atlanta, 1997 *Küstner*

Frank Edwards

If it ain't been in a pawnshop, it can't play the blues.

Don't none of these record companies believe in paying nothing much. Most of them are deadbeats, cheaters, and swindlers. They don't pay nothing, but they make good money.

Born in 1909 in Washington, Georgia, **FRANK EDWARDS** actively performed his blues for nearly eighty years, from 1923 until his death in 2002. He had fond memories of his grandparents, both of whom had been slaves. He bought his first guitar at the age of twelve. His father was a strict Christian and forbade Frank to play and smashed his instrument. Frank left home at fourteen after he argued with his father about the feeding of their mules. A group of his cousins were going to Florida to find work and Frank went with them. He never returned home. In Florida he found work and bought another guitar. He befriended Tampa Red, "Champion of the Slide Guitar," in St. Augustine in 1926. After a few years, Frank got the urge to travel and spent the rest of the twenties and thirties hoboing across the United States honing his craft.

He began performing on the streets and made good money. He performed and lived with Tommy McClennan in Mississippi for six months. It was McClennan who took him to Chicago and introduced him to record producer Walter Melrose who recorded his first 78s. In Atlanta he was friends with blues greats Blind Willie McTell, Curley Weaver, and Buddy Moss.

He recorded for the Okeh record label in 1941, for Regal in Atlanta in 1949, and later made an album for Trix, in the early 1970s.

I met Mr. Frank in 1995 and even though he had not been performing much, even in his hometown of Atlanta, he played great and MMRF began finding performance opportunities for him. Shortly thereafter, we began producing a CD for Mr. Frank. Over a few years we recorded two sessions and were close to completing a great album. He began to travel to big shows with MMRF and play often in Atlanta. He wrote new songs and contacted me to inform me that he was ready to finish his record. The day after his ninety-third birthday he visited us in Hillsborough. The morning of the session he ate a big breakfast then sat down with Cool John Ferguson on the drums and recorded seven new compositions. Convinced his album was complete, he decided to return home. While a friend was driving him to Atlanta, the angels came and took him away.

One of his favorite songs was his wry original "Chicken Raid":

If a preacher should come around
Catch a bus and get out of town.
He'll eat you out of house and home—
Pluck the chicken, leave the bone.

Atlanta, circa 1940 *Photographer unknown*

Pinnacle, North Carolina, 1999 *Duffy*

Cool John Ferguson

The guitar has always intrigued me and I had to find out what it was about. I knew I had to learn how to play it and it just came natural to me.

1996. Duffy

In 1998 **JOHN FERGUSON** began to use his talents to support the efforts of the Music Maker Relief Foundation. He has helped make classic recordings for Essie Mae Brooks, Carl Rutherford, and Captain Luke as well as his own debut album. John can execute any style of music flawlessly. He is among the finest blues guitarists alive today.

He was born on December 3, 1953 on Saint Helena Island off the coast of South Carolina. His mother is of the Gullah people and John grew up with the old ways all around him.

Cool John has been playing the guitar since age three, learning to play by listening. His first guitar was a Harmony #1 with a one-coil pick-up, two knobs, and a Marvel amplifier. He still remembers the shape and look of it and the way it made him feel. At five he was playing church music professionally, often out-seating musicians ten times his age. For three years he was a featured entertainer on *The Low Country Sing* on Channel 5 Charleston TV, appearing with his three sisters (The Ferguson Sisters), a popular gospel trio. He was also featured on stage every morning at school, where the principal found that live music kept the students civilized before the start of class.

In the seventh grade he was a mainstay of his high school band and chorus. Around this time he began what was to be a lengthy association with Earl Davis, his music teacher. John became a fixture in the band room, where Earl taught him music theory and charting and John learned to play every instrument in the room. In the tenth grade John formed his first band, the Soul Connection, playing rhythm and blues at school functions. In his junior year he attended the first integrated high school class in Beaufort and formed an integrated band, the Plastic Society, venturing into psychedelic pop music and beginning to play club dates.

Throughout this time John played guitar and piano at a minimum of two church gigs every Sunday. One day an itinerant preacher rolled into Beaufort in a rusted-out '49 Chevy. His name was Reverend Ike and he soon set up shop at the United House of Prayer on the corner of Duke and Haymore. He hired John for a two-week gig and immediately attracted large crowds with his peculiar philosophy of personal empowerment through cash donations for Ike's nascent broadcast empire. "You can't lose with the stuff I use" was a favorite catchphrase.

John pulled his weight and then some. "I brought in just as much attendance as he did," John said. "Chicks would see me play at the honky-tonks and then come to hear me in church." As Ike's popularity grew and he traveled to preach in ever-larger venues, he took John on the road with him, to Macon, Savannah, and as far west as the Houston Coliseum.

He graduated from high school in 1972 and with his mentor formed the Earl Davis Trio with Earl on sax, Earl's wife on organ, and John on guitar, playing jazz. This began an extremely active period for Cool John. He took on a house gig at the Latai Inn at Fripp Island Resort and was playing four churches on Sunday. His next gig lasted five years, with Stephen Best and the Soul Crusaders, playing black clubs throughout South Carolina. This was followed by a long solo engagement at the Sans Souci in Beaufort, playing dinner jazz interspersed with blues, soul, and rock.

"I always gave them a little more than they wanted. When it was time to beef things up I knew where to go." He played the Sans Souci four nights a week and it was there, at twenty-seven, that he was married to his wife Brenda. In the years since, John has traveled where the music has taken him, equally comfortable in churches and clubs. He has been active on the tent revival circuit and has been associated with LaFace Records of Atlanta, collaborating on pop recordings with his niece Esperanza.

John epitomizes the traditional role of the musician as an integral entity in the everyday life of the community. Through his work in the church he has provided the soundtrack for thousands of weddings, funerals, picnics, and parties. He and his sister Bessie made something of a specialty of funerals, working closely with the director to dictate the appropriate tone of the event. "He would say, 'Let them cry, but not too much, then let the spirit out.' I would come out with some sad stuff, then unexpectedly cheer them up. And a lot of them would come to see me at the club I was playing that night."

The man breathes music and plays from the inside out. He commands the rare ability to develop a theme on the fly, incorporating every element of the situation along the way and somehow summing them all up neatly when he feels the end coming. His improvised pieces carry the aesthetic sensibility of careful, painstakingly crafted works, which in fact they are; it is simply all done in real time.

—WESLEY WILKES

St. Helena, South Carolina, 1996 *Duffy*

Northside Tavern, Atlanta, 1999 *Austin*

Jesus heard me praying. I bowed down under the pecan tree.
"Jesus, if you freed my soul let it rain." It rained.

Cora Fluker

CORA FLUKER was born in Livingston, Alabama, around 1920 to a family of sharecroppers. The conditions were so hard that she tried to run away at the age of nine only to be caught by the white landowner and beaten nearly to death. She has scars on her back and is deeply haunted by this awful memory. Many years ago on her praying ground under a pecan tree by her house in Mississippi, she had a vision of Jesus and thenceforth devoted her life to preaching. When she sings and preaches, her voice has the power of a saxophone.

Marion, Mississippi, 1996 *Küstner*

Marion, Mississippi, 1996 *Duffy*

Walnut Cove, North Carolina, 1994 *Hoppe*

Preston Fulp

I didn't make any money at moonshining. Liquor wasn't about fifteen cents a pint and wasn't no money in it. I swapped liquor for eggs and give them liquor and things like that. That was back in the thirties, about Hoover time. The law didn't bother you back then. The county did not want to feed you if they brought you in.

Born in 1915, **PRESTON FULP** grew up in Walnut Cove, an area just north of Winston-Salem, North Carolina, where his family sharecropped tobacco. Preston took to music at an early age, starting to play the guitar when he was six. By his teens he was proficient on the violin and banjo and was a singer of both blues and hillbilly songs. He also played blues with local musicians such as Wheeler Bailey and Arthur Anderson and listened intently to the 78 RPM records of Blind Blake and Blind Willie McTell. He played hillbilly music with Ernest Thompson and Vernon Covenant and with Carter Family and Uncle Dave Macon records. Soon he was performing in both styles on Saturdays at corn shuckings, chicken stews, and barn dances. He recalled a dance hall he played regularly in neighboring Mount Airy. The black and white people were segregated and he would go to one side of the hall and play mountain music for the whites and then go to the other side and play blues for the blacks. Preston was unique in this ability to perform both styles of music.

Preston often performed at the tobacco auctions in Winston-Salem. These were great events, as it was the time of year that farmers had cash from the sale of their crops. In the fall for three months every year, the streets would fill with barkers, moonshiners, soapbox preachers, medicine men, and musicians, all hawking their goods. Working all week at the sawmill, Preston would make $4.50 and then perform at the auction houses all night Friday and Saturday, often coming home with $100. During the Depression, Preston, seeking better times, hopped a freight. He found farm work throughout the Midwest and up into Canada, where he became a friend with a potato farmer. Here Preston stayed and worked in the potato fields and taught his new friend the art of moonshining. Five years later Preston hoboed back to Walnut Cove. While jumping off the last boxcar near his home, he fell and broke his left arm.

Frustrated that he could not play guitar, he peeled back the plaster from his fingers just enough to fret the neck, then propped the guitar body on his left knee and continued to perform. He held the guitar in this manner the rest of his life. By this time the elder blues musicians had drifted off and Preston played hillbilly music with banjo players and fiddlers. Preston never left Walnut Cove again. He married, settled down, and supported his family by growing tobacco and working in a sawmill.

Preston had a haunting falsetto voice and intricate East Coast guitar style. He loved music and would spend the spring, summer, and fall sitting on a chair in his car-port with his guitar, singing and playing to his grandchildren and neighbors and friends who passed by. A neighboring farmer once told me that when the tobacco-curing time came around, his father would get Preston's guitar out of the pawn shop and Preston would sit and play until daybreak, song after song.

Charleston, South Carolina, 1992 *Hoppe*

I've played so much guitar,
it would make your ass hurt.

Guitar Gabriel

GUITAR GABRIEL was an authentic blues troubadour and a walking encyclopedia of blues and gospel, knowing literally thousands of songs. He performed an eclectic mixture of gospel and Piedmont, Chicago, and Texas blues styles, all done in his own gritty, Piedmont-rooted idiom that he called Toot Blues. Guitar Gabriel <u>was</u> the blues! He was a man of words, an imaginative guitarist, and a heart-wrenching singer.

Guitar Gabriel was born Robert Lewis Jones in Atlanta on October 12, 1925. He moved to Winston-Salem, North Carolina, at the age of five. His childhood memories were of his life on the farm which his father sharecropped. While growing up, music was part of his family life. He was raised by his great-grandmother, an ex-slave who lived to be one hundred twelve and played the banjo and called set dances. His grandmother played the pump organ and his grandfather played the banjo. His father and uncle were blues guitarists and singers. All of his sisters were exceptional gospel and blues singers.

In 1939, his father, Sonny Jones, traveled to Memphis with Blind Boy Fuller and Sonny Terry to record some records on the Vocalian label. In Baltimore, Jones made a record in 1950 on the Orchid label. After leaving the farm for good, Jones worked as a laborer and on

Wearing his original hat *Duffy*

WHEN I MAKE OTHER PEOPLE HAPPY, THEN I AM HAPPY. About music—it keeps you out of violence. Blues is special because it takes a lot of animosity out of your heart. Like, if you have a misunderstanding. Instead of taking violence out with your fists, you take it out on your music. If you get disheartened you take the guitar and you can satisfy yourself and that takes all [the] evil thoughts away from you. That is what music is all about. That's the bottom of it. When you can do that you are all right and you got something to fall back on. If you can't play no music, sing, or dance, and all you can do is think, you got to do something to take that pressure off. If you drink that drink, [it] is going to make you violent and you have no choice because you have nothing else to turn to. You got to have an outlet. If you can get to the thing you love, it is going to take that evil heart away from you. That is about the bottom line on me.

Music is a difficult thing if you do not understand it. Music is a feeling. If you can't feel what you are doing, you can't do it. If you don't like what you are doing, you are not going

weekends he entertained at chitlin struts and fish fries. He was nicknamed Razorblade because he dazzled the crowd not only through his music but also by eating razorblades, Mason jars, and light bulbs. Gabe never learned his father's tricks, yet from listening to his father's music, he became obsessed with the guitar. He fell asleep every night with a guitar wrapped in his arms, exhausted from learning his father's two-finger blues guitar style.

When Gabriel was ten, his father took a job in Durham, North Carolina, as a laborer helping build Camp Butner, a P.O.W. camp. The family lived in the Hayti district in a rooming house above a funeral home. Too young to work construction, Gabriel ventured out to the streets with his guitar. This is where he first met and played with Piedmont blues legends Blind Boy Fuller and Reverend Gary Davis. At the age of fifteen, Gabriel left home and hoboed to Atlanta to stay with his grandmother, where he continued to perform on the streets. When Gabe returned home at eighteen his father heard him play his old steel guitar. Gabriel played so well that his father gave him the guitar. Gabe soon left, traveling with his new instrument, now a qualified bluesman.

When World War II broke out, Gabriel served his country in the army. When he returned to the United States, African-American youth was bopping to the blues. Gabriel soon left Winston-Salem and toured Nashville, Detroit, St. Louis, New Orleans, Chicago, San Francisco, Los Angeles, New York, Baltimore, Philadelphia, Miami, and other cities playing his music.

In the Deep South he found refuge from racism in show work. He began with old-time medicine shows, the first being one owned by an old Cherokee man named Chief Wahoo. Gabriel would play the guitar and draw a

Sam Red's drink house, Winston-Salem, North Carolina, 1993 *Küstner*

to do it. You can do it, but you won't be good at it. Like a preacher. You take a city preacher, he'll say, "Ladies and gentlemen. . . ." No one wants to hear that shit. You get one of those old country preachers—he will start screaming. He is doing it from his heart. See the main thing is reaching the audience. Make them feel what you feel. Once you do that you are all right. Other than that . . . you might as well hang it up.

I'm good but I don't brag it. I am not afraid to get in front of anybody. I know I am good. When you know something, you do not have to ask nobody. As long as I feel it in my heart that I am good, I am good.

Guitar Gabriel's story is taken from interviews conducted by Timothy Duffy, edited by David Nelson, and first published in Living Blues, *May/June, 1992.*

crowd, allowing his boss to pitch his patent medicines. Later, he was hired as a musician with the Dixie Classic Fair and that is where he took the stage name Guitar Gabriel. The seven-piece band played Dixieland, blues, and marches in the big top. At midnight the admission price was raised, the tent cleared of children, and the musicians played the blues to accompany the exotic dancers in the burlesque show. After several years with the fair, he headed his own band named Guitar Gabriel and the Troubadours. During the winter months he hoboed and played from town to town.

In 1970, Gabriel, then known as Bobby Jones, lived in Pittsburgh. There he recorded a 45 of his song "Welfare Blues" and an album, My South/My Blues on the Gemini label. The producer, Bill Lawrence, gave Robert the name Nyles (alluding to the Nile River). The 45 became a number-one hit in Pittsburgh and Cleveland and Nyles Jones became a local legend. A review in Blues Unlimited magazine proclaimed it the most important single of the year. He began playing blues festivals with artists such as Reverend Gary Davis, Mance Lipscombe, Son House, Lightnin' Hopkins, and Arthur "Big Boy" Cruddup.

Times were good for awhile but then, never realizing any royalties from sales of the 45 or album, he became disgusted with the music business. Disheartened by this incident, he returned to his native South.

Throughout the seventies Gabriel lived in Winston-Salem and played his music at black clubs and for gospel groups. By the eighties he stopped all club and church work. He walked the streets with his guitar, playing for his friends at drink houses and for the children getting off their school buses. He was known by his entire community, having raised many of them with his music.

In 1988 the French record label Jambalaya reissued

Winston-Salem, North Carolina, 1992 *Duffy*

the LP *My South/My Blues* as *Nyles Jones, The Welfare Blues*. Once again people began wondering who this mysterious man was.

MMRF located Guitar Gabriel in March 1991 after hearing about him from bluesman James "Guitar Slim" Stevens of Greensboro, North Carolina. With the foundation's help, Gabriel immediately put out a cassette entitled *Toot Blues*. Gabriel and his back-up band, Brothers in the Kitchen, began performing frequently at clubs and festivals. He appeared overseas for the first time at Blues Estafette in Holland in 1991. Gabriel went on to perform at festivals in Belgium, Switzerland, Canada, and throughout the United States, including performances at Lincoln Center and Carnegie Hall.

Gabe died April 2, 1996, just as he was being afforded the recognition and acclaim the world had withheld for so long. His spirit was strong but his body destroyed by a life lived hard. He is with us today in the mission of the Music Maker Relief Foundation—to seek out his extant peers in the blues community and bring their talents to the fore while they still survive.

Port Townsend, Washington, 1995 *Duffy*

Winston-Salem, North Carolina, 1995 *Duffy*

With Mother Pauline, Ridgeway, South Carolina, 1998 *Duffy*

God brought me a mighty long ways. He woke me up this morning and started me on my way. He didn't have to do it, but he done it.

Elder James Goins

ELDER JAMES GOINS, born July 18, 1921, is pastor of the Spiritual Holiness Church in Simpson, South Carolina. He and his wife Mother Pauline often perform together. Their music, described by Taj Mahal as "electrifying," is a combination of ancient African musical traditions and early African-American gospel sounds.

Pinnacle, North Carolina, 2000 *Duffy*

The blues is the cold, hard truth.

Macavine Hayes

MACAVINE HAYES was born in Tampa, Florida, on June 3, 1943. His family farmed and he was the oldest of five sisters and five brothers. He remembers, "There was always something to do down on the farm, we listened to the radio and got up on the back porch and played the music of Chuck Berry and Jimmy Reed."

In the sixties, he met Guitar Gabriel playing on the streets of Tampa. He followed his new friend back to Winston-Salem, North Carolina. "Gabe taught me how to experience the road, sleep outside, go to some gal's house and spend the night sometimes," Macavine said. "Go to church on Sunday, we always carried nice suits and shoes. We would look good. We did a lot of travelin'. We went to Atlanta, down to Augusta, and all through Florida. We played at juke joints and lay a hat down. Gabe was a free spirit and taught me that you can go anywhere you want to go. We ran a drink house together for years down on Claremont Street. Living with Gabe was not a hard life—you just had to drink all the time."

Richard "Big Boy" Henry

RICHARD "BIG BOY" HENRY is the Carolinas' premier blues shouter. He was born in 1921 in Beaufort, a small fishing village on the North Carolina coast. He has worked as a fisherman, preacher, and blues singer since the early 1940s. Big Boy plays the Piedmont blues that was created by Blind Boy Fuller and the musicians surrounding him in Durham, North Carolina—a blues with more upbeat strumming and finger-picking, even ragtime influence, than its Delta counterpart.

Beaufort, North Carolina, 1993 *Duffy*

"Old Bill"

You know, I'm sitting here thinking about a few years
When I was a little boy, I used to have a rooster called Old Bill.
He would sleep in my windowsill and he would always follow me
Wherever I would go, he would follow me.

So, I heard my mother talking one Sunday morning, you know.
You know, she's a Baptist woman, she loved to wear them big
     hats, you know
Dress up, you know.
I heard her tell my pappa
She said, "Listen, old man we are going to fix Old Bill.
We're going to cook Old Bill this morning."
I said, Oh Lord
You know, the preacher coming and the preacher got to have
     some chicken.
I said, Lord they're going to kill Old Bill.

They're going to kill Old Bill
This morning, soon.
Whoa, they're going to kill Old Bill
This morning, soon.
Old preacher going to eat Old Bill
Carry Old Bill to his lonesome home.

Momma got up, Daddy got up
I had a pretty mother
The old man was jealous, he always kept a gun behind the door,
Preacher come and stay with us
Sometime when my daddy wasn't there.
The old preacher would come in and asked my mother one day
     to give him a holy kiss.

She said, "No, no, no, old reverend. No, no. My husband'd kill me.
    I can't do that."
I was watching. I would watch everything around there.
But I looked out in the yard and I saw Old Bill and I said,
Now they are going to kill Old Bill for that old preacher.

Daddy got up early this morning
Grabbed Old Bill and wrung his neck.
I heard Bill try to holler, "Don't do it, don't do it!"
But it was too late.
Lord, have mercy
They done killed Old Bill.
Bill won't come around the door and get no more crumbs.

They killed Old Bill
This morning soon
Whoa, they killed Old Bill.
Killed my rooster this morning soon
Old preacher got Old Bill
Done carried Old Bill to his lonesome home.

So that Sunday the preacher was sitting around the table
They stewed Old Bill and put pastry on him.
Mother said, "Come on, son."
I said, no, no, no, no,
I can't eat my rooster.

Duffy

Old preacher stood to the table—
He liked to eat the whole rooster
Sitting there picking his teeth, telling jokes and lies to my daddy.
After awhile he decided to get ready to go home
Catch the bus
He said, "I'm going to see you all in the next go-round."
I see he looked at my mother and gave her a smile
Mother turned her head
She knew the old man was watching.
I ain't kidding
The old man would have hit the side of the old preachers' head.
But anyhow old preacher left, started down the road
Tears come rolling down my eyes

They killed Old Bill
Old Bill ain't here no more.
Whoa, they killed Old Bill
Old Bill ain't here no more.
Preacher got Old Bill
Old boy going on down the road.

Good-bye Bill, good-bye.
That's the story, the story of Old Bill
My little red rooster.

Farmville, North Carolina, 1997 *Küstner*

George Higgs

GEORGE HIGGS was born in 1930 in a farming community in Edgecombe County near Speed, North Carolina ("a slow town with a fast name," as he is fond of saying.) He learned to play the harmonica as a child from his father, Jesse Higgs, who enjoyed playing favorite spirituals and folk tunes at home during his spare time. George got to hear the medicine showman and harmonica player Peg Leg Sam playing locally in Rocky Mount during the annual tobacco market season and he made a lasting impression on the young harp player. Higgs was attracted to the guitar as a teenager and reluctantly sold a favorite squirrel dog to a neighbor to raise funds to purchase his first. As a result of their close proximity, the dog spent more time at George's home than at his new owner's, so Higgs got to have both the guitar and the company of his dog.

—LIGHTNIN' WELLS

from "I Won't Be Back No More"

I'm going away to leave you, I won't be back no more
Well I'm going, I'm going, where the chilly winds don't blow.

Sun rises in the east, until it sets up in the west
It's hard, hard to tell which one I love the best.

Bye-bye, baby, if I never see you no more
Well I'm going, I'm going where the climate suits my clothes.

Tarboro, North Carolina, 1998. *Duffy*

Middlesex, North Carolina, 1998 *Austin*

Algia Mae Hinton

If you kill a chicken, save me the head.

Middlesex, North Carolina, 1996 *Küstner*

ALGIA MAE HINTON was born on August 29, 1929, in Johnston County, North Carolina. Her parents, Alexander and Ollie O'Neal, were farmers who raised tobacco, cotton, cucumbers, and sweet potatoes. Mother Ollie could play many stringed instruments and began teaching Algia when she was just nine years old. She was the youngest of fourteen children and worked the fields from an early age. Her musical and agricultural upbringing set the stage for her adult life.

Algia married Millard Hinton in 1950. Her husband died in 1965, forcing Algia to raise her seven children alone by working long hours on the farm. Despite these trying circumstances, Algia kept the music alive and passed it on to her children. Together, they fought off the hard times by entertaining the people of their community. Over the years Algia's music has gained international recognition.

—Lightnin' Wells

Middlesex, North Carolina, 1999 *Duffy*

On a throne by Sam McMillan beside Donna Smith,
Pinnacle, North Carolina, 1998 *Austin*

Carl Hodges

CARL HODGES of Saluda, Virginia, was born in 1931 and is among the few Chesapeake Bay blues artists performing today. In true songster tradition he performs blues, country, and gospel songs sung with his old-time vibrato-laden voice.

from "Flossie"

Flossie, what's the matter?
She has gone to Cincinnati.
She's a rounder, in heart, oh Lord,
and she's gone with that $10,000 man.

Durham, North Carolina, 1998 *Küstner*

John Dee Holeman

JOHN DEE HOLEMAN was born in Orange County, North Carolina, in 1929. He is a storyteller, dancer, and a blues artist who played with musicians who had learned directly from Blind Boy Fuller. He possesses an expressive blues voice and is a wonderful guitarist incorporating both Piedmont and Texas guitar styles. A recipient of a National Endowment for the Arts National Heritage fellowship and a North Carolina Folk Heritage award, John Dee has toured the U.S., Europe, and Asia. John recently retired from a career as a heavy machine operator and continues to tour both in the States and abroad.

"When John Dee and I sat down and played together the experience was like coming full circle back to my roots! His music took me straight back to a gentleman named Lynwood Perry in Springfield, Massachusetts, the only person I ever learned to play guitar from. As it turns out, Lynwood was also from Durham, North Carolina. It was like meeting up with an old friend! John Dee Holeman is a carrier of the southeast guitar tradition."

—TAJ MAHAL

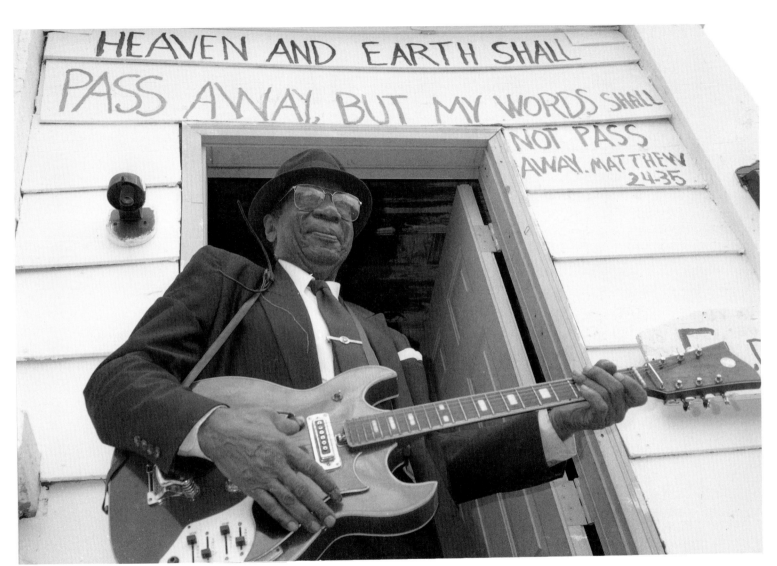

Newport News, Virginia, 1997 *Duffy*

Elder Anderson Johnson

I used to shine shoes in front of a barber shop, that is when I made enough money to buy my first guitar. I sat down and played and made so much noise that my mother ran me out of the room and I had to go and hide someplace to play.

ELDER ANDERSON JOHNSON was born in 1915 on a farm seventy miles outside of Richmond, Virginia. Beginning at age eight, he spent his career preaching and playing his steel guitar on the streets of America. He made a fine record of "God Don't Like It" and other songs back in 1958 in Miami for the Angel, Glory, and Deluxe labels. He eventually settled in Newport News, Virginia, where he consecrated his church, later called the Faith Mission, in the first floor of his house. "I never tried to build churches, I try to build my faith," Anderson said. "That is what has gotten me through, my faith. I have never been in trouble in my life, because my faith has kept me going." He became a respected outsider artist, his paintings mainly of women's faces. He loved to play his steel guitar and sing but was also a fine pianist and drummer. Elder Anderson died in 1998.

Newport News, Virginia, 1997 *Küstner*

MY GOD DON'T LIKE IT

So many people say they cut whiskey out,
But let them have a little wine,
But they get on a drunk every once in a while,
They must be drinking moonshine.

CHORUS
God don't like it,
I don't either;
It's a sin and a shame.

2
So many people get on a drunk every
    once in a while,
Just to speak their sober mind,
But when they're caught up it is a trap,
They put that blame on shine.

3
This country's going to be lost
If it keeps on the way it's going;
We can't have a church in town,
For the preachers all drinking moonshine.

4
The preacher went to the sister's house,
She asked him to rest his hat,
He began to laugh and grin,
"Sister, tell me where your husband's at."

5
Some of these sisters in the churches
Used to where their dresses so short
The people had to talk,
But now they're wearing them so long,
They can hardly walk.

6
I know you don't like my song,
I spoke my sober mind,
I won't take back a word I said,
Because I don't drink moonshine.

Composed by

Elder A. Johnson
2807 Madison Avenue
Newport News, Virginia

Elba, Alabama, 1993 *Küstner*

David Johnson

DAVID JOHNSON (1930–1997) lived in a cinderblock house without electricity or running water in the country outside of Elba, Alabama. He was a musician and a visionary outsider artist. In the 1940s and 1950s David traveled by bus from Michigan to Mexico as a street musician singing and playing his harmonica.

He had a small pet pony that he could hitch up to a great assortment of buggies that he had crafted by hand. His yard was full of sculptures of airplanes and cars. David loved to talk, often telling of his latest invention. A concrete statue of a cowboy that David made watches over his grave, proclaiming, "Here rests a unique kind human being."

Johnson's house, Elba, Alabama, 1995 *Küstner*

With Taj Mahal (*right*), New Orleans, 1997 *Duffy*

Ernie K-Doe

ERNIE K-DOE had a huge novelty hit with the R&B song "Mother-in-Law" in 1961. He and his wife Antoinette opened their own club, the Mother-in-Law Lounge, in New Orleans in 1995 which remains a popular stop for musicians coming through town. Ernie had been through the mill, but with the help of his wife he regained his dignity and some well-deserved recognition towards the end of his career. MMRF helped him by providing small grants in times of emergency. He nicknamed himself the Emperor of the World and when he passed away in 2001 New Orleans honored him with the largest funeral parade in years.

"Ernie K-Doe's music was some of the best New Orleans music I ever heard. What excited me most about him was his vocal style, the way he raised his notes at the end of the line. He always sang positively about what he was singing about. K-Doe and I talked about it and he was surprised that I listened that close. He is a big factor in the way I sing my words today."

—TAJ MAHAL

Winston-Salem, North Carolina, 1994 *Küstner*

Pernell King

from "Late in the Evening"

I walked in the rain, 'til my feet got
    soaking wet.
I walked in the rain, Lord have mercy,
    'til my feet got soaking wet.
Well, I been walking all night, have
    mercy Gabriel,
I ain't found my baby yet.

PERNELL KING from Winston-Salem, North Carolina, is a half-brother of Guitar Gabriel. In their youth the pair hoboed the country playing their blues. Pernell spent twenty-seven years in prison. Gabe would often visit with him while he was out on work crews. He had a beautiful smooth voice and Gabe would bring out his guitar and they would sing right there on the side of the road. He was finally set free and he and his brother spent a good deal of time with one another playing their blues down at Ezelle's drink house.

With Ezelle and Hawkeye and Ezelle's drink house, Winston-Salem, North Carolina, 1996 *Küstner*

King at microphone with Travis Hodge and Willie James Williams at the Freedom Creek Blues and Gospel Festival, Old Memphis, Alabama, 1999 *Küstner*

Willie King

When you start hollering some blues, you can feel the blues going away in the wind. That is how I get the blues off of me, because if you don't, the blues can take you down. I mean under. It can get on you so heavy. The blues won't bother you if you howl the blues. It keeps hard times off of you, you don't have a penny in your pocket but you feel good.

WILLIE KING lives in Pickens County, Alabama, just a few miles from Mississippi, several miles from Aliceville. He envisioned and created a nonprofit organization called the Rural Members Association to teach young people their heritage and what he calls survival skills.

"We see these kids now, they got all the problems we had coming up—dealing with the oppressor; figuring how to survive; feeling their self-worth under attack; success around them most always wearing a white face unless it's the preacher's and most time he just content to have his fine clothes, nice car, a church where they come, and there on the wall is a blond Jesus," King says, explaining his reasons for forming RMA. "These kids, they got nothing to do. They mess with gangs, with drugs; they got no family teaching them their traditions, the African-American traditions. No tie to the land, the crafts of survival we always practiced in the country; no time for the blues. Now, you can be poor—and ain't nobody likes to be poor— but when you lose your culture you lose everything.

"We take kids out to pick wild berries and wild plums and we teach them to make jellies and preserves. We preserve figs, peaches, and pears. We teach them how to make quilts and do wood work. Then we come down to the music—the blues and the gospel music. This is set up to pass on the traditions. We teach them the basics of how to play the guitar, bass, and sing and write songs. We give guitars and amplifiers to the ones that really show an interest."

Rural Members Association students, Freedom Creek Blues and Gospel Festival, Old Memphis, Alabama, 1999 *Duffy*

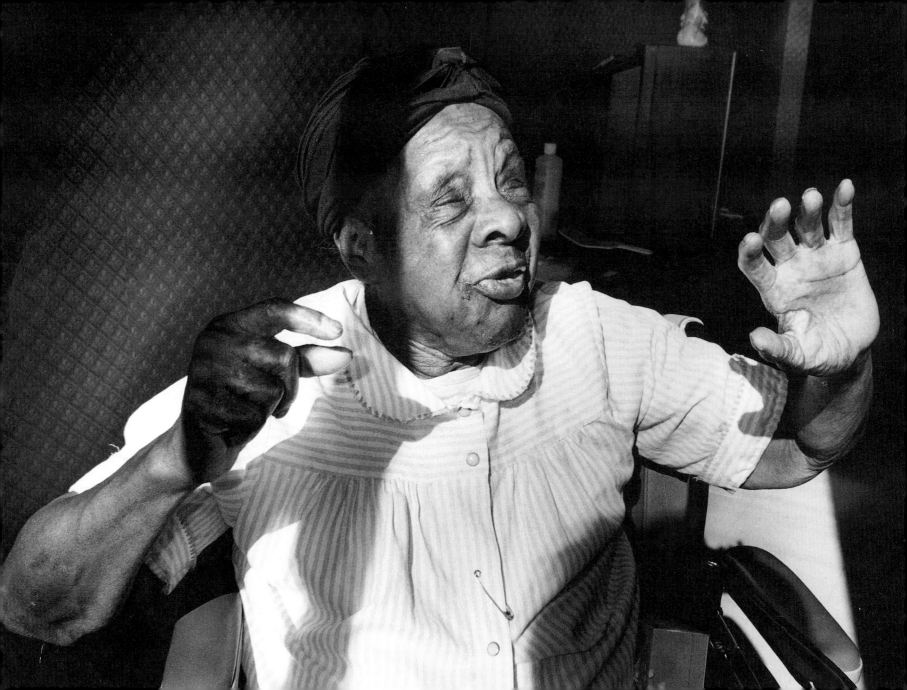

Lucille Lindsay

I asked Guitar Gabriel one day if he had any brothers or sisters. He mentioned that he had a sister but he had not seen her in eight years. He gave me her married name, **LUCILLE LINDSAY**, and I found her, blind from diabetes, in an awful nursing home. When I reunited this pair the next day they immediately broke into song. I scrambled to put up my recording equipment as they sang. Gabriel had written a spiritual the day their mother passed away. Their emotions were so intense that they both began crying and their tears soaked the fronts of their shirts.

I went through the mill and I'm still going through it, but one of these days I will be where I can rest in peace and won't have to do nothing but fly around, just fly around heaven all day. Oh my God won't that be wonderful, just fly around with those beautiful wings, just fly around heaven all day. Nothing to worry about, you don't have to worry about no food, no bills—Lord have mercy.

Winston-Salem, North Carolina, 1995 *Duffy*

With Willa Mae Buckner, Winston-Salem, North Carolina, 1998 *Austin*

Taj Mahal

Born in 1942, **TAJ MAHAL** grew up in Springfield, Massachusetts, and learned to play the blues at age thirteen from neighbors who had recently migrated from Mississippi and North Carolina. This musical giant is at ease performing country blues, ragtime, reggae, rhythm and blues, jazz, folk, Caribbean music, and the music of West Africa. As a young adult he worked on a dairy farm, and received a degree from the University of Massachusetts in animal husbandry. In 1964 he started performing in the Boston folk music scene and in 1965 he moved to Los Angeles where he began his seminal career as a recording artist. His first three albums for Columbia are considered classics and have been used as blueprints for generations of aspiring musicians. Taj is loved and respected by musicians of every genre throughout the world.

Roanoke Rapids, North Carolina, 1995 *Duffy*

Bishop Dready Manning

BISHOP DREADY MANNING, born in 1934, lives in Roanoke Rapids, North Carolina, where he is the bishop of the St. Mark Holiness Church. Bishop Manning is a former bluesman who long ago dedicated his music to songs in praise of the Lord.

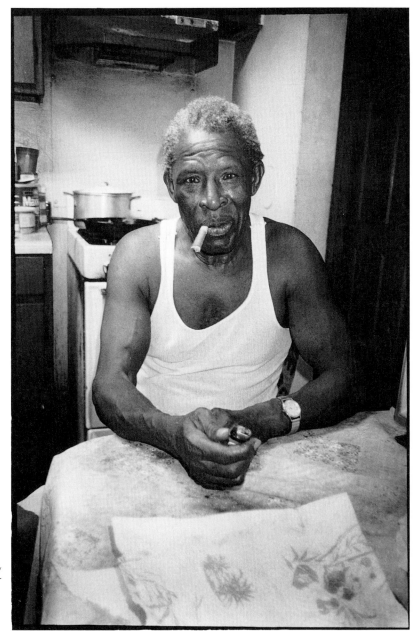

Winston-Salem, North Carolina, 2000 *Duffy*

Luther "Captain Luke" Mayer

LUTHER "CAPTAIN LUKE" MAYER was born in Greenville, South Carolina, in 1926. He grew up on his grandparent's farm in nearby Clinton, where he followed the furrows barefoot behind the plow as his Uncle Jesse worked and sang to his mule. Luke's ambition at the time was to learn to drive a mule. It was one he never achieved, but he soaked in the music of the countryside as Jesse played his harmonica on the evening porch.

At fourteen he moved to Winston-Salem, North Carolina, with his mother and sister, where the exigencies of the situation carried him increasingly out of school and into the workforce. At seventeen he went to work for LaSalle Bell, a junkman who demanded a full day's work from his young employee. LaSalle was a large man and Luke soon learned to lift his own end of a scrap motor and heave it onto a flatbed truck without pause or complaint. Early on he had developed a talent for imitation, and Luke began to sing the songs he heard on the radio, everything from the big band singers to hillbilly ballads. "Back then I had eleventeen voices," he has said.

Captain Luke was blessed with a deep natural baritone. He was accustomed to carrying the low parts in his church choir, and his abilities soon caught the attention of Otis King, who taught him how to hold the

Winston-Salem, North Carolina, 1998 *Küstner*

low notes and make them rise and fall. Soon Luke was singing bass professionally in King's Gospel Quintet. He also began to entertain at informal gatherings, an avocation that would endear him to friends and strangers alike throughout his life. Accompanied by whatever instrumentation available, Luke would travel in a wide circle from Winston performing in drink houses, the social hubs of the African-American community in the North Carolina piedmont. His repertoire changed with the popular music of the changing times and grew to include comedy routines, notably renditions of Amos 'n' Andy skits with inflection-perfect renditions of every character. He worked continually, raising four girls and two boys in Winston-Salem. In 1969 he moved to New York City and worked for four years in the garment industry until called back to Winston for a family emergency. He has remained there since.

A chance encounter in the early seventies led to a long association with Guitar Gabriel. Gabe was a master of the country blues, another musical form that suited Luke's voice perfectly, and the two became fixtures in the Winston-Salem drink-house scene, alongside such local luminaries as Macavine Hayes, Whistlin' Britches, Willa Mae Buckner, and Mr. Q. Sometime early in this period an admiral's hat in Miller's Variety Store caught Luke's eye and in an instant he became Captain Luke. Although completely unfamiliar with boats, Luke was a leader of men by anyone's standards: the handle fit and it stuck.

Captain Luke's body has been sculpted by a lifetime at labor. His formative years under the scrap-metal tutelage of Mr. Bell built biceps that fifty years later bulge from his sleeveless shirt like a young athlete's. The thick roped muscles of his arms ripple as he lifts a cigar from his mouth, then relax as his arms hang

Winston-Salem, North Carolina, 1998 *Küstner*

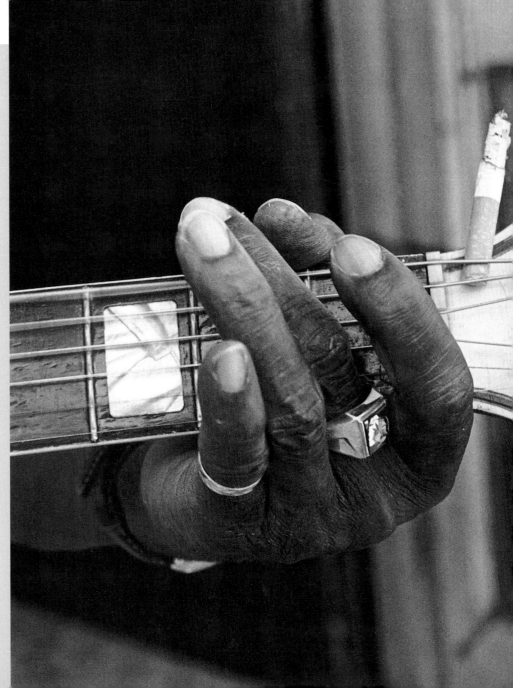

loose and his dark face cracks into a wide smile. Answers to questions come easily to Luke. His uncommon combination of youthful demeanor and ancient wisdom are perhaps born of his direct approach to the contingencies of everyday life.

Luke's music and art are rooted firmly in the African-American working class of the Carolina Piedmont and the mystique of his message refers continually to the blues experience. However, as a pure entertainer in the milieu of the drink houses, Luke's style and song selection have periodically changed to suit the needs and desires of his audience. The average blues listener—at the moment predominately white—naturally supposes these to be the standard popular forms of the thirties and forties.

In the real world the community has its own criteria. In his current collaboration with guitar wizard John Ferguson, Luke explores the broad ranges of the idiom, from its roots in the deep country (let it not be forgotten that country music has borrowed heavily from African-American forms), all the way to it's modern pop/showbiz manifestations. From the simple nursery rhyme "Old Black Buck" to the more familiar sounds of Lightnin' Hopkins and Guitar Gabriel through the rhythm and blues of Joe Simon to the sentimental songs of Billy Eckstein and the last great master of the genre, Brook Benton, Luke's rich dry baritone provides a panoramic tour of his musical influences.

His sound is an unusual convergence that might best be called Outsider Lounge Music, basic and sophisticated in the same moment, that speaks to us with the savage perspicacity of Satchmo in his prime and swings with the easy grace of a young Dean Martin.

—WESLEY WILKES

Gadsen, Alabama, 1995 *Duffy*

Jerry "Boogie" McCain

JERRY "BOOGIE" MCCAIN is the greatest harp player alive today. In his seventies he remains at the height of his powers, constantly writing and delivering amazing live performances with the energy of a teenager. Born in 1930 in Gadsden, Alabama, Jerry began playing his harp and singing along with jukebox records at his father's barbecue stand, the Green Front Café. He began recording in the early fifties for the Trumpet label making records of his unique blend of country swing and down-home blues. In 1955 he recorded for the Excello label and has continued making great records to the present day.

"Viagra Man"

Let me do it baby
Oh, little girl I know I can.
Oh, let me do it Mama
Oh, little girl I know I can.
I'll give you love when you want it
No matter how long you want it.
I am the Viagra Man.

I ain't worried about getting up, mama
and I sure ain't worried about falling down.
I ain't worried about getting up
and I sure ain't worried about falling down.
I am the Viagra Man
And they're talking about me all over town.

Don't have no mercy on me
Cause I ain't gonna have none on you.
Don't have no mercy on me, woman
Cause I ain't gonna have none on you.
You're gonna run on down to the projects
And say that man did everything he said he'd do.

I STARTED PLAYIN' HARMONICA WHEN I WAS FIVE. My daddy used to own a barbecue stand called the Green Front Café. And he had a jukebox. I'd be on the outside, cuttin' wood, you know. I would hear these blues on the jukebox. Arthur "Big Boy" Crudup, Brownie McGhee, all these people, Sonny Boy Williamson. And I said, "I'm gonna make me a record." I would be out on the corner, people come around, and I'd be playin' blues, but I'd play a lot of little boogie tunes. Everytime I'd be out on the corner, a guy'd say, "Hey, Jerry, play me one of them little boogie things," you know, and so I'd do that all the time. So they just started callin' me Boogie.

As I was growin' up—I was fifteen, sixteen, seventeen, eighteen—the police would always stop me and want me to play harmonica. They'd want me to play the thing called "Put the Dog in Behind the Rabbit" and "The Foxtrot" and all that stuff, and "The Train." And I got sick of "The Train" and "The Dog Runnin' The Rabbit." And so one day they pulled up 'side of me and said, "Hey, Boogie, come on and play me a tune." And so I said, "I ain't got my harmonica." I ain't gonna play for 'em today. He pulled up beside me, said, "Get in." I get in the car and they take me home, and I get out, run in the house just like I'm goin' to get the harmonica and come back out, you know, and play for 'em. Man, they just worried me to death. I got sick and tired of it.

When Little Walter came out with "Can't Hold Out Much Longer" and "Juke," I was dead on it. I just went crazy over it. 'Cause of the mellow tones. He's an innovator, he's the one that started all this amplified jive, you know. Yeah, man. He came through here, he was playin' right down the street there. Big club, black club. I met him down there, told him who I was.

And he loved that corn. My brother, he knew all the bootleggers and he used to haul white liquor for people, you know. So Little Walter came in and we got together and he wanted to go find some corn. So we got to ridin' around and the thing that Little Walter had out 'bout "You Know I'm Just Crazy 'Bout You Baby, Wonder Do You Ever Think of Me." I changed it. I'm

sittin in the back and he and my brother sittin' up front. I said, "Little Walter Said He Was Crazy 'Bout You Baby, Wonder Did You Ever Think of Him." And I was in the back, workin' on the harmonica. I said, "But You Know Little Walter Didn't Know, Old Jerry Was the Cause His Light Burnin' So Dim." And, boy, he just went crazy. He said, "Man, you come up on stage. I'm gonna let you play tonight." And, boy, the place was just like that. And they were just jumpin' and dancin'. So he beckoned for me and I went up on stage and he handed me the harmonica right quick and I just kept on playin' and they had danced a long time, they thought it was still Walter, you know.

Some of 'em can talk to me, like you and I can be talkin' and you could say one phrase, two words, I say, "Oh, hell, that's a song." And I write what you said down and then I go from there. I used to go up to a guy who was a bootlegger at a motel, he had rooms up there, special rooms where people'd go to drink and these girls would come from a little old place over there called East Gadsden, and they would come over there and buy wine and stuff and they used to just buy me wine because I'd just be rhymin'. They'd say, "Make up one about this leopard coat." Bam, bam, bam, bam. Just like that, boy. They just sit back: "I don't know how in the world you do that." Drinkin' that ol' cheap wine called Red Mustang. They just loved to hear me talk. When I write a song I want it to tell some kind of a story. Just like "Burn the Crackhouse Down," you know, "Sue Somebody." I was sittin' here watchin' television and seen all four of them black women sittin' up there, this one want $6,000 from Mike Tyson, this one want $4,000. I'm sittin' there, "Man, all them women want to sue Mike Tyson." I said, "Damn, everybody want to sue somebody." I said, "Oh, shit." Then I got up and got my pencil. When I write a song, it's got a meaning behind it.

—*FROM AN INTERVIEW WITH DAVID NELSON WHICH FIRST APPEARED IN* LIVING BLUES, *FEBRUARY 1994.*

With Ardie Dean and Denise Duffy, Atlanta, 1998 *Austin*

Charlotte, North Carolina, 1994 *Hoppe*

"Diamond Teeth" Mary Smith McClain

"DIAMOND TEETH" MARY SMITH MCCLAIN was born in 1902 in West Virginia. After running away from home at thirteen, Mary toured the chitlin circuit as an acrobat and singer with such troupes as the Davis S. Bell Medicine Show and Irwin C. Miller's Brown Skin Models. Mary shared the bill with such greats as Count Basie, Cab Calloway, Ray Charles, Nat King Cole, Sara Vaughn, and Fats Waller. Bessie Smith was a big-sister figure to her and the two performed with the F. S. Walcott Rabbits Foot Minstrel Show. Mary had diamonds (from a bracelet her step-mother gave her or from a necklace she stole from the abusive woman, depending on the story) inserted into her teeth as a publicity gimmick in the forties. During the leanest of times, the diamonds were replaced with tinfoil and once the diamonds were pawned to pay for her mother's medical care. At the end of her life, friends in her adopted hometown of Tampa Bay, Florida, helped her have new diamonds installed. Willa Mae Buckner told me that when she first joined a traveling show Mary was one of the biggest stars of the day. Amazingly the two were reunited to perform at Carnegie Hall together in 1995. She died at age ninety-eight and her ashes were spread along the railroad track in her natal town of Huntington.

"Our favorite act was 'The Lady with the Million-Dollar Smile,' F. S. Walcott's big featured singer, who'd come on in the third quarter of the show. She was an armful. She wore bright dresses and had all her teeth filled with diamonds! She sang on all those real get-down songs like 'Shake a Hand.'"

—LEVON HELM, THIS WHEEL'S ON FIRE

Perry, Georgia, 1999 *Duffy*

Rufus McKenzie

RUFUS MCKENZIE was born to a sharecropping family in Perry, Georgia, in 1927. As a child he worked in the cotton fields, singing to his mule to pick up the pace. Rufus reflected, "I learned my music through sadness and coming up hard. I had to wear white people's worn-out shoes. I had little clothes to wear."

from "Mother Sleep On"

Sleep on, sleep on, mother as I pray
I hope to see, see your smiling face again one day.
Sleep on, mother sleep on
When the gates of heaven open wide I hope to be there,
    staring you in your eye.
Mother sleep on as I pray I hope to see you face to face
    again one day.

—RUFUS MCKENZIE

With Lucas Duffy, Pinnacle, North Carolina, 2001 *Duffy*

I belong to the old Primitive Baptist church. We do not have any instruments in our church. We make our music with our mouth and our feet.

Nora Millner

I was born in December 27, 1918, in Wilkes County, North Carolina. I had a white daddy and a brown-skinned mama. My daddy was from well-to-do people but he never owned up to me and I never saw him. My mother was Lilly Wards. I was put out in other people's homes when I was eight years old. I could cook and I could do most any old thing. I started digging out in the fields at the same time. I got married in 1938 and we started sharecropping and I worked out on the farm until I was sixty-eight years old. I have been on Roby and Besse Fulk's farm since I was twenty years old—I'm still on that farm. We are family. I then started working as a caregiver out in a neighbor's home. I can pray the fire out of a burn or cure a baby of thrush and stop bleeding. I can do these things because I never laid eyes upon my father.

Pinnacle, North Carolina, 1998 *Duffy*

The blues lifts me up when I'm down.

George Herbert Moore

GEORGE HERBERT MOORE was born in 1929 in eastern North Carolina in the town of Burgaw. George worked hard manual labor in the fields and sawmills during his life. Music Maker Relief Foundation was able to provide him with a good guitar.

I play blues all by myself. I don't need a band. I can play all day and all night. I don't get tired. The music I play will take you way back, that is what I can do.

Taylor Moore

TAYLOR MOORE is from Paulette, Mississippi, and he plays deep blues from his home back in the country. When Taylor plays his music, it's hypnotizing, and extremely primal. He will tell you that the melodies he plays come from the air.

With his wife, Old Memphis, Alabama, 1999 *Duffy*

Old Memphis, Alabama, 1999 *Duffy*

Bentonia, Mississippi, 1995 *Küstner*

Jack Owens

JACK OWENS (1904–1997) was a farmer his entire life in the small town of Bentonia, Mississippi, where he ran a juke joint at his home on weekends. Ethnomusicologist David Evans met Jack during one his research trips in the sixties. Since that meeting hundreds of blues fans made the pilgrimage to Jack's door. Folklorist and well-known maker of field recordings Alan Lomax visited him once and encouraged Jack to keep playing his guitar in his unique minor tuning. When I visited him in 1995 he had taken that advice to heart and he played only in this unique Bentonia style. Later that year I arranged for him to go on his first trip abroad to a festival in Utrecht, Holland. Because he had no birth certificate or other ID, it took great efforts to get him a passport. Eventually, an older relative was found who could swear in an affidavit as to Jack's identity. Jack and his escort finally arrived at the airport only to have Jack detained because he had a pistol in his boot. Somehow he made the flight and got to the show.

from "Keep On Grumblin'"

Keep on grumblin', lowdown way I do
Keep on grumblin', baby girl, lowdown way I do.
If I put you down, pretty girl, treat me the same way I do.

When she was leaving, wouldn't even wave her hand
When she was leaving, baby girl, wouldn't even wave her hand.
That's alright, baby girl, one day you will understand
One day you will understand.

Oh baby girl, bring your clothes on home
So I mean, baby girl, bring your clothes on home.
Don't you think you done me, baby, think you are doing me
    wrong
Leave poor Jack at home.

When she was leaving, baby, I said stop your lowdown ways
Couldn't you, baby girl, quit your lowdown ways.
I could have quit you, baby girl, and your lowdown ways.

Bentonia, Mississippi, 1995 *Küstner*

Charlotte, North Carolina, 1998 *Duffy*

Neal Pattman

Nobody makes moonshine, works a cakewalk, chops wood, or plays a harmonica like seventy-something **NEAL PATTMAN**. Losing an arm in a wagon wheel at the age of nine hasn't slowed him at all. "Sixty-six years ago the blues knocked on my door and they wouldn't leave," Pattman said. His testimony can be heard in a sound and a style his father taught him as a child in the country outside his hometown of Athens, Georgia.

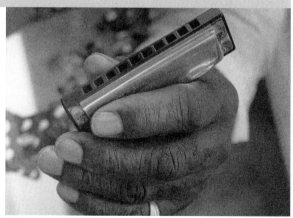

Charlotte, North Carolina, 1998 *Duffy*

from "Prison Blues"

If you ever want to do a crime
You'd better stop before you make up your mind.

Six months on the road, you know, it ain't no time
I'm doing one to ninety-nine.

Wonder, who's loving my baby tonight?
Wonder, who holding her by her hand?

Kingston Mines, Chicago, 1998 *Austin*

Portraits and Songs from the Roots of America

With Guitar Gabriel (*left*),
Port Townsend, Washington, 1995 *Duffy*

Joe Willie "Pinetop" Perkins

When you're born down in Mississippi, you've got the blues even if you can't sing 'em.

JOE WILLIE "PINETOP" PERKINS was born in Belzoni, Mississippi, in 1913. As a young boy he witnessed the legendary Blind Lemon Jefferson perform at his school on the Stovall plantation. Pinetop started as a guitar player and after being cut in his left arm with a knife by an outraged chorus girl in the mid-forties he switched to piano. Perkins played with singer and slide guitarist Robert Nighthawk, playing on Nighthawk's KFFA radio show in Helena, Arkansas. He was later invited by harp legend Sonny Boy Williamson to appear with him on the *King Biscuit Time* radio program. Like many Delta musicians he migrated to Chicago where he was fortunate to replace Otis Spann in Muddy Waters' band in 1969. Guitar Gabriel and he ran into each other at a blues festival and they were both happy to see one another as they used to play together in the fifties on Maxwell Street in Chicago.

Eugene Powell

EUGENE POWELL was born in Utica, Mississippi, a small town about twenty-five miles southwest of the state capital of Jackson, to Rosie Powell, a black domestic worker. His father was the white Homer Powell. This gave Eugene an ambivalent status among both races. While still a young boy, Eugene lost his right eye to a hostile youngster's bow and arrow—done on purpose, not as an accident while playing as is usually reported. He only met his father once—he gave the boy a gun.

When Eugene was eight, at home in the Delta at Lombardy, Mississippi, his mother ordered a guitar for him from the Sears and Roebuck wish book—three days later he was playing it and soon started entertaining the guards at nearby Parchman prison farm together with his brother Ben on mandolin. Eugene began to play at picnics and suppers. During the late 1920s, Eugene worked as an itinerant musician in Mississippi, the Arkansas Delta, Tennessee, and Louisiana. Playing for both blacks and whites, he delivered whatever his audience requested—blues, popular music, and ragtime pieces.

It was during this time that he met guitarist Richard "Hacksaw" Harney (1902–1978) who influenced

On his porch, Greenville, Mississippi, 1996 *Küstner*

Play it a long time, 'cause a short time will make me mad.

Eugene's playing heavily (as did the records of Blind Lemon Jefferson, Blind Blake, and Lonnie Johnson). Other musicians he knew well during those years were members of the musical Chahron family (Bo, better known as Bo Carter; Sam; and Lonnie—all performing as "The Mississippi Sharks"), Walter Vinson, guitarists Mott Willis, Robert Nighthawk, and Houston Stackhouse, as well as many other, more obscure musicians from the Greenville/Hollandale area.

Eugene waxed his first recordings for the Bluebird label on October 15, 1936, at the St. Charles Hotel in New Orleans. At this session, co-produced by Bo Carter, Eugene made six recordings as Sonny Boy Nelson; backing him on second guitar was Brother Willie Harris. They both also played behind Eugene's girlfriend Mississippi Matilda (1914–1973) singing four songs, and harmonica player Robert Hill on ten tracks, a variety of blues and popular tunes. Sixty years later Eugene could still recall the whole group traveling from the Delta by car to the session but winding up in the opposite direction in Pascagoula, Mississippi—a truck driver finally leading them into New Orleans. He also remembered that photos were taken of the musicians and claimed that he earned about six hundred dollars for these recordings.

At that time Eugene made his living sharecropping but also operated a roadhouse where he would earn money gambling and selling bootleg liquor and homebrew.

By the early 1950s Eugene and Matilda separated (she moved to Chicago with their eight children) and the amplified blues that was then emerging gave artists like Eugene fewer and fewer opportunities to perform. Upon the urging of his old friend Sam Chatmon, Eugene got back into music around 1970. But unlike many of the other rediscovered bluesmen, who were then performing mostly for white audiences, Eugene never really participated in the era's so-called blues revival. Instead, he stayed home in Greenville, feeling obliged to take care of his disabled girlfriend Carrie. Just because somebody wore out, you don't throw them away, he told writer and photographer Val Wilmer in 1972.

That year, however, he made a rare appearance at the Smithsonian Festival of American Folklife in Washington, D.C., where he was reunited with his old playing partners "Hacksaw" Harney, Sam Chatmon, and Houston Stackhouse. After Carrie's death, more appearances followed, usually at the annual Delta Blues Festival in Greenville and the Sunflower Blues Festival in Clarksdale.

In 1994 he actually married for the first time—to Lois Eva Smith of Hollandale, Mississippi, a woman about half his age.

One couldn't meet a more welcoming, friendly, and communicative man than Eugene. He certainly enjoyed company and sharing his musical skills and view of the world with anybody interested in listening—it was nothing unusual for Eugene to sit down and talk non-stop for five hours about his long, hard life. Yet it is sometimes impossible to imagine all the things he (and most other people in the Delta) had to go through in order to survive.

—Axel Küstner

Winston-Salem, North Carolina, 1991 *Hoppe*

Sam Red

I have operated a drink house in Winston-Salem since 1945. I never have had any problems. Guitar Gabriel, Guitar Red, Washboard Sam, Guitar Slim, Macavine Hayes, and many others played in my house.

SAM RED has run a drink house for over forty-five years in Winston-Salem, North Carolina. Drink houses in Winston's black community, like juke joints in the Mississippi Delta, remain a vibrant setting for the perpetuation of the blues at its most real and rooted level. A refuge for the homeless and the down-and-out, as well as a gathering place for friends and lovers, the drink houses are on-going house parties where emotions run high, alcohol flows heavy, and the music is raw.

—DAVID NELSON

Winston-Salem, North Carolina, 1995 *Duffy*

Jahue Rorie

When I first came to town I played for three days against Guitar Gabriel trading back and forth seeing who knew the most blues. He did put me down, but we always remained good friends.

JAHUE RORIE was born in 1936 in the country outside of Charlotte, North Carolina. Jahue has a great repertoire of Lightnin' Hopkins, Arthur "Big Boy" Cruddup, and Blind Boy Fuller songs. He has been following bluesmen playing in North Carolina drink houses since the fifties.

War, West Virginia, 1996 *Küstner*

Carl Rutherford

CARL RUTHERFORD is a master guitarist, singer, and Dobro player who blends the styles of traditional mountain, gospel, blues, and country music. Born in War, West Virginia, in 1929, Carl learned guitar from his Uncle Will at the age of eleven. After working in the coalfields of the Olga Coal Company until 1950, Carl moved to California and performed at honky tonks in an around Bakersfield, California. After twenty years out West, Carl moved back to his beloved mountains of West Virginia. From "Love Can't Fly on Broken Wings" to his hypnotizing instrumental "West Virginia Breakdown," Carl's music expresses his life and love for his mountain culture.

War, West Virginia, 1998 *Küstner*

IT'S A GRAY WORLD AND NO YELLOW LINE, snow falling harder now. The road to Mayberry twists slick and mean once Winston-Salem recedes in the rear view. There is no Mayberry, of course. It's really Mount Airy. Mount Pilot, also of *The Andy Griffith Show* fame, is really Pilot Mountain, and you can see it from the exit to Pinnacle, North Carolina. On a clear day, that is, you can see it. This is not a clear day.

The slow ride to the Music Maker Relief Foundation headquarters and recording studio leads to a steep drive, and there at the top is Carl Rutherford's van, cased in ice, cold clothes strewn all over the interior. Next to the van is a cabin, and inside the cabin are three men, two with guitars and one without.

Carl Rutherford is sitting on a chair, holding one of the guitars. He's wearing a flannel jacket lined with quilted polyester. Just now he reaches underneath his chair, coughing as he roots around in his bucket of medicine bottles in search of something he says is a nebulizer. A nebulizer blows compressed air, turning Carl's medication into a fog to inhale.

"It's breathin' treatment," he says. "Gettin' some of that shit out of my lungs."

That's the shit that he says is going to kill him, and he figures it'll happen before too long. This is Carl Rutherford's last recording session, so far as he can tell. He's moving to California to be with his daughter. Moving to California to get out of the cold. And to die.

Carl used to live in California, but he's originally from War, West Virginia. He pronounces some words sort of like Loretta Lynn does, even though she's from Kentucky. He knows about coal mining and about organizing workers. He knows how to praise God. He's known all of this for a long time.

"God stacked War just as steep as it could be stacked," he says. "You try to do anything with that land, you're going to have trouble. They're little spike hills. Stick up like spikes."

He has all these songs, Carl does. Hank Williams would be proud to sing some of these songs. "Love Can't Fly On Broken Wings." Hank would have liked that one. "Flyin' High, Walkin' Tall," too.

Then there are the ones about the mines. "You've got to turn off the fear, when you come down into here," he sings, and that's when you know he never really left them. Carl Rutherford saw bad things happen down there: "A man's life ain't nothin'/ Lordy, that's how it seems." That's War he's talking about. "You gotta pray that the dear Lord is holding you near."

That's for real, from a man who went to a week of funerals after a catastrophic mining accident. After that, the cage man got pissed off when Carl held up the coal show by vacillating, going back and forth about whether or not he could go back down into the mines.

"Finally, my dad said, 'If you don't go now, you'll probably never go in again.' We'd just bought a strip of land, so I said, 'I need to stay and work and help pay that off.' I made sixteen dollars a day. When I got the money saved, I was gone. I went to California."

These songs, this life—lived mostly in West Virginia and California, in coal and in timber and in music—are swirling around inside the cabin like the snow swirls outside of it. John Ferguson sits next to one wall, listening to Carl, smiling sometimes, playing along. Ferguson is world class. "I don't believe I've ever heard nobody any better than this fella," Carl says. "God, he plays so pretty."

"I was at a state gathering in West Virginia, and somebody said, 'Carl, make a blues tape,'" he remembers. "I said, 'What is blues?' They said, 'Carl, you are blues.' I said, 'Okay, then I can do that.'"

Pinnacle, North Carolina, 1999 *Duffy*

Not so much gets done today. The bass player shows up, then leaves, scared that the snow will keep him from getting to Asheville in time for a paying gig.

Little spurts of brilliance, marred by out-of-tune guitars, recording glitches, or harmony singers who can't sing loud enough—that's what happens today. But the little spurts are something else.

Ferguson is all over Carl's album. Listen to what they played together. "I will cling to the old rugged cross," Carl sang. You could hear Carl breathe when he's not singing. Carl breathes loud. Ferguson set notes on top of each other, building little pyramids of vibrato, little stepping stones to something once out of reach. "I will cling to the old rugged cross," Carl sang, and that's clinging for real. "And I'll exchange it someday for a crown." That's hope and belief, which is all we've got, unless you count this life.

True-life hillbilly blues and mountain gospel. Little shards of California honky-tonk.

"Ain't that something? One pass," Carl said after he and Ferguson finished up with one of these.

One pass, that's all.

If you want to know who Carl Rutherford is, you can listen to Carl's album *Turn Off the Fear*. If you want to know where he's been and what he's done, you're going to have to ask around West Virginia and California and Tennessee and all the other places where he's said or sung something that moved people to feel and act differently than they did before.

Carl is someone entirely different. He's steeped in folklore, in mystery, in coal dust and rallies and jukeboxes.

War, West Virginia, 1998 *Duffy*

He thinks he knows the deal with "In the Pines." He knows about the fellow who wrote it.

"My dad knew all that, from where he grew up," he said. "It's about what they call the Pines, outside of Caryville, Tennessee. Out from Knoxville. "In the Pines" was two deaf mutes. She's a gorgeous thing, and they got to courtin'. He worked on a section gang. There was a wreck down the line somewhere, and the train's running way late. Real long sucker. She was going to the post office, and didn't know the train was running late. He was waving at her, and it didn't do any good. It hit her.

"Then he went crazy. Went off into the caves there that they called the Pines. About two years later, somebody found his bones in the cave. The poems he wrote was beside of him. Then there was a medicine man come through that picked the banjo and sold the black draught. Somebody gave him the poem, the words, and he set the melody to it."

Carl sang better in the shadow of Pilot Mountain than he'd sung in years. The reflux was under control ("I found a doctor in West Virginia who knew how to control that stuff. I was sounding like Louis Armstrong before that."). His back-up was up to the task at hand, and the task at hand was getting Carl's songs down right.

That meant creating the soundtrack to a real American life. His coal-mining songs are a lot like love songs. Hell, coal mining *is* love. Bad love, at least. Crunched down into a dark, fearful place, breathing in the shit that's gonna kill you. Good love is different, but it's harder to happen upon. And none of it matters if the Bible is for real.

—PETER COOPER

Winston-Salem, North Carolina, 1996 *Küstner*

Cuselle "Mr. Q" Settle

I said to myself one night, hell, I got ten fingers, I can play too. I started going to my aunt, who had one of those self-playing pianos, and my first song was Earl Hines's theme song, "Rosetta." I learned how to play that just like he played and, shoot, I would get a job.

Mr. Q, as he's known, was born **CUSELLE SETTLE** in 1913. He is an old hep-cat whose music just makes you have to smile. A self-taught pianist, he has fashioned his own sound by mixing the piano styles of Art Tatum, Earl Hines, and Oscar Peterson interspersed with songs by the Ink Spots.

He graduated from North Carolina A&T in the thirties. He started his career when he left school to travel with Blanche Calloway's Orchestra as a singer. They performed as far away as Mexico; traveling back through Texas he took off on his own and hustled a job as a singer in a local saloon. When he returned home six months later his parents were upset. Mr. Q appeased them by giving his mother five hundred dollars he earned in tips, all in change. He soon migrated to Harlem and got a job playing harmonica with the Savoy Sultans, the house band at the Savoy ballroom. He went to all-night jam sessions where he heard the legends of the day such as Oscar Peterson, Art Tatum, and Teddy Wilson. Mr. Q returned to Winston-Salem in 1963 and became a fixture performing at local piano bars.

Pinnacle, North Carolina, 1998 *Duffy*

Pinnacle, North Carolina, 1999 *Austin*

Drink Small

I was born in 1933 in Lee County in Bishopville, South Carolina. I started playing when I was eleven years old. We had an old pump organ; I started playing "Coon Shine Baby" on that. Then I started on the one-string guitar; I played "Bottle, Up and Go." My uncle had a guitar around and I fooled around on that. I made my own little guitar, for strings I cut up an old inner tube.

When I was in high school I organized a group called the Six Stars. I was ashamed to sing; I was playing instrumental songs like Blind Boy Fuller stuff. I played piano in the church. Then I began to start singing. I came up playing both blues and gospel. On Friday and Saturday night I would make five dollars a night playing at house parties. That was more than a man plowing a mule all week was getting.

I then went to school to be a barber but I did not want to cut no hair—I wanted to cut up.

I became a great guitar player. I joined the Spiritualaires. We recorded on the Vee Jay label. When we broke up, I came back to Columbia, South Carolina, and I started to play for the college kids and they went wild. I recorded "I Love You Alberta" and "Cold, Cold, Rain" on the Sharp label. They call me the Blues Doctor 'cause I can play all the styles—bottleneck, ragtime, Piedmont blues, Chicago Blues. I can tear them up. I am the Blues Doctor.

from "Widow Woman"

Widow woman get lonesome sometimes
She needs a man to give her a little peace of mind.

Widow woman, sleeping by yourself
Sometimes you want to be with somebody else.

Widow woman get lonesome late at night
She needs a man to come around and hold her tight.

Widow woman, she's all alone
She needs a man to call her very own.

Some people say that a woman that has got a house full of
    children is not lonely.
She looks in the mirror and powders her face and she says,
"I got a eleven head of children, but the children don't under-
    stand
Nothing takes the place of good old country man."

Widow women, I want to say something to you all—
If you want a good man call on the man they call Drink Small.

Columbia, South Carolina, 1999 *Duffy*

Rembert, South Carolina, 1997 *Duffy*

Albert Smith

ALBERT SMITH was born in Rembert, South Carolina, and began playing the piano in 1927 when his parents bought him one from the Sears and Roebuck catalog. Albert is a soft-spoken man who in his nineties remains a powerful blues shouter and barrelhouse pianist. Albert has remained in his county his entire life, never traveling far from home. Albert has been the inspiration to countless younger musicians such as Drink Small who grew up his neighbor. When MMRF went to visit him we took him a new piano as his old one just would not stay in tune.

from "Walk On, Walker"

Walk on, walker; talk on, talker
I know you are talking about me,
But the more you walk and the more you talk
The Lord is going to take care of me.

You see that old liar, she gets out on the streets and she talks
    to the first person she meets.
Well she's talking about you and she's talking about me
Everybody's business around in town
Going to lie until the sun comes up, until the sun goes down.

If you was the right sort, I never would have thought
A big-mouth person likes to talk anybody's business around in
    town,
Is going to lie until the sun comes up, until the sun goes down.

Winston-Salem, North Carolina, 1991 *Hoppe*

Joe Smith

JOE SMITH helped run Sam Red's drink house in Winston-Salem, North Carolina. He used to hawk Chief Wahoo's medicine oil back with Guitar Gabriel when the tobacco market was a real spectacle. One afternoon Gabe and he told me their old pitches and we made up a label. Joe showed me how to make the Healing Oil and Guitar began to sell it at our shows. It was great fun and you would be surprised how many letters we got testifying to the curative powers of our product.

Chief Wahoo's Healing Oil is Jerusalem magic, direct from Haiti! It is good for rheumatism, aches and pains, back and knees, depression, gout, corns and calluses, sleepless nights, migraine headaches, also for the neck and your libido.

A man could not drive his truck, he had a sore leg. I said, I will make medicine. I put him back to driving a truck and a car too. The doctor couldn't do him no good, but I could.

Cambridge, Massachusetts, 1999 *Duffy*

from "Money Blues"

Tell me, little girl, where'd you get that gold?
Costs so much money; you don't want to pay.
Where you been, little girl? You been getting' it everyday.

Henry Spencer

HENRY SPENCER was born December 9, 1926, in Switchback, West Virginia. As a young boy Henry began performing on the harmonica with his father Roy Spencer, a coal miner. When he was a teenager, Henry began hopping freight trains because he wanted to see the world. At the age of eighteen he joined his father working in the mines. In the early 1950s Henry was drafted into the army and experienced combat in Korea. Returning from the service he settled in Boston, where his family had relocated. In the 1960s there were many bluesmen performing in Boston and Henry often performed with J. B. Hutto and Luther "Snake" Johnson at nightclubs such as the Speakeasy, the Patio Lounge, and the 1369 Jazz Club. "I play from the heart. God gave me this, and I can go into a church and rock it just like I go in a club and rock it if I want to," Henry says.

Greenville, South Carolina, 1997 *Duffy*

Cootie Stark

"I took a lot of abusing off of people in this life," says **COOTIE STARK**, sitting in the passenger seat of a station wagon that is taking him back to the Woodland Homes public housing projects in Greenville, South Carolina.

"I been through the hassles, man. And a whole lot of phony talk, you know. Phony talk. But I kept on, and I got to that smooth road. You ain't gonna get there if you think getting to the smooth road is easy. That's in life. Something is better out there for you. Sometimes when we get disgusted, we have to just try to hold on."

Cootie's smooth road is still fraught with surface scars. He is a poor, blind, seventy-six-year-old man who draws disability checks and lives alone in a ghetto apartment. Or else he's a forgotten hero of the blues, a direct link to Piedmont acoustic legends Pink Anderson, Simmie Dooley, and Baby Tate, an artist of international stature and unquestionable importance.

It all depends on who you ask. It all depends on who you believe. Cootie Stark appears in none of the accepted blues historians' books. Until recently, he was unknown, undocumented, unheard. But MMRF has taken Cootie to Europe, a cigarette company presented Stark's face to 3.5 million people in the form of a

With Beverly "Guitar" Watkins and Neal Pattman, Austin, Texas, 1999 *Duffy*

million-dollar ad in *Rolling Stone*, and a CD is out that makes all the scholars look like phony talkers.

"I'm happy about all that, man," Stark says as the car stops in front of his apartment. "I ain't never had it before, so it makes me happy. There's a lot of people still living that want to hear this, and they ain't got it on the radio. It should have been forty-five years ago, but more likely I'm better now than I was in my twenties. More likely I'm better."

Cootie Stark was born James Miller, but most everyone in Anderson County, South Carolina, called him Johnny. Some of them called him Cootie, though he can't remember exactly why. He worked in the cotton fields with his sharecropper parents and dreamed of playing music for a living.

Visits to an aunt in Greenville when Cootie was twelve presented him with the Piedmont blues influences that root his guitar style today.

"Greenville had good talent back then," he said. "Baby Tate used to play on the street there, and that's how I come to know him. Then I got a guitar when I was fourteen, and I learned songs from my Uncle Chump and a bunch of songs from Baby Tate."

Cootie was encouraged to keep playing, in part because his near-total blindness was considered an impediment to ever working a straight job or gaining an education.

"There was a man came to my momma's house when I was a teenager," Stark says. "He talked to Momma about me coming to the Spartanburg school for blind people. I wanted to go, but she didn't let me. Back in those days she thought they might be mean to me. That's the reason why."

Three years after picking up the instrument, Cootie Miller was playing street corners in Greenville and square dances in the outlying counties. He began what

Greenville, South Carolina, 1996 *Küstner*

he calls his "traveling years" after turning twenty, performing on the streets of Asheville, Knoxville, Greensboro, Columbia, and other Southern cities and playing with elder musicians who would one day be recognized as blues legends: Pink Anderson, Simmie Dooley, Peg Leg Sam, and Josh White.

But while Tate, Anderson, Dooley, Sam, and White each recorded music that still endures, Cootie remained in unrecorded obscurity, moving from town to town, playing for whatever he could get.

"People would talk about, 'Oh, he got a good gift,' but all they knew was to give me a drink of liquor or a nickel or a dime or two," he says. "They didn't have the learning to really help me."

The details of Miller's next forty years are nebulous, a hazy continuum of struggle and song. If there were few missed opportunities it is because there were few opportunities of any sort. Rock and roll obliterated the way America thought about popular music. Then the folk boom of the 1960s brought first-generation blues artists like White, Anderson, Reverend Gary Davis, and Lightnin' Hopkins briefly into the national spotlight, though music scholars declined to bestow much significance on second-generation players who extended and honored the idiom's traditions.

Miller married twice and saw one union broken by death, the other by divorce. He moved back to Greenville in the 1980s, settling into Woodland Homes with little hope of ever finding an audience.

"By then, the real Piedmont blues was pretty much gone," he says. "All them guys was dead and gone, and I wasn't making no headway."

It was in the spring of 1997, Tim Duffy traveled to South Carolina and saw Cootie Stark play electric guitar and sing Fats Domino songs.

"I realized by the way he was playing the guitar that there was something more there than a Fats Domino copycat," Duffy says. "I started asking Cootie, 'Do you know any older songs?' He said, 'Oh, you like those old songs? I had an uncle named Uncle Chump and I knew this guy named Baby Tate. He taught me thousands of songs. You want to hear some of those?'"

Within months of hooking up with Duffy, Cootie had a new acoustic guitar, a new stage name (Stark was the last name of Miller's stepfather) and a promising career. The biggest obstacle in the early part of the Cootie Stark/MMRF alliance was convincing Cootie that getting paid good money for playing music didn't mean he would lose his disability check. A former duo partner told him he couldn't make more than one hundred dollars on a gig without repercussions.

"Yeah, I told Timmy about the situation I was in with the governor," Stark remembers. "He checked on it for me, and then he said, 'If that's all you're scared about, you don't have to worry.' That's when we went to New York and I started out with him, and we've been going around together ever since."

MMRF's notion that most traditional blues clubs provide a poor way to turn a buck or garner attention means that its artists are more likely to play Carnegie Hall or the Newport Rhythm and Blues Festival than to appear on small stages. And, whether playing European shows, American festival gigs or a toney jewelry store in the Hamptons, Stark has been

universally well-received as an international blues figure. His abrasive, percussive guitar style melds with a vocal arsenal that ranges from a rough-hewn gospel shout to a tight, pretty vibrato, and his concerts are glorious time warps, direct links to a South long since gone.

"They say the older you get, the more fun you gonna have, and I believe them now," Stark says. "I just wish I'd had some of this a long time ago. I've had a lot of wasted time, a lot of time gone. But that was just an old, bumpy road."

—Peter Cooper, excerpted from "Payback Time," *The Oxford American*, Summer, 1997.

With Neal Pattman and Mudcat Dudeck holding Lucas Duffy, New York, 1997 *Duffy*

With Jonny Lang and Tim Duffy, Berlin, 1998 *Küstner*

Performing at a picnic, Gray, Georgia, 2000 *Duffy*

On his porch, Greensboro, North Carolina, 1982 *Küstner*

James "Guitar Slim" Stephens

JAMES "GUITAR SLIM" STEPHENS was born on March 10, 1915, in South Carolina. He began to play the pump organ at the age of five and two years later he switched to piano. In his early teens he joined the John Henry Davis Medicine Show. He soon picked up the guitar, an instrument which he truly mastered. It was his welcoming spirit that opened the doors of the Carolina blues, a world rarely seen by outsiders, to MMRF.

Blues will be popular as long as the world stands. It'll take away any other musician you may come up with. Them ol' blues is just a natural-born killer and they always have been, 'cause they come from slavery on up, you understand?

Asheville, North Carolina, 1997 *Duffy*

Samuel Turner Stevens

I used to go back in the mountains and hand these old banjo players a fretted banjo and they would pick it up, admire it, and then hand it back to me. They played fretless banjos. It's from these old-time musicians that I got the idea to start building my own fretless banjos and learning to play these old tunes.

SAMUEL TURNER STEVENS
(1925–1999) made beautiful fretless banjos, fiddles, guitars, mandolins, wooden mallets, canoe oars, telescopes, windmills, rifles, lamps, sleds, chairs, and was an award-winning pool player. His curiosity for life was infectious.

His neighbor was the great song collector and founder of the Asheville Folk Festival Bascombe Lamar Lunsford. Sam would drive with Bascombe deep into nearby Madison County. They would work for a farmer all day in the fields and in exchange the man would sing them the old ballads, some of them from his mother, also a singer. Sam was also a leader in the old shape-note singing gatherings, camp meetings in which four-part folk hymns are sung in an *a cappella* style dating to the 1840s.

Asheville, North Carolina, 1999 *Duffy*

Henry Stewart

In 1983 I rented a small cabin in the mountains above Asheville, North Carolina, for thirty-five dollars a month. After living there a couple of weeks I began to hear beautiful singing and harp music coming from the woods above me. This went on for a few days until I decided to walk up the hill and find out who this was. Sitting on an old well was **HENRY STEWART**. His family lived on top of the ridge just as they had since they moved there 150 years before. Henry and his family befriended me. I began working for them digging fence postholes, and I spent many afternoons behind the barn with Henry, playing guitar as he sang old country and gospel songs and blowing his harp.

I was raised up here on this mountain and I never have lived anywhere else. My mother is 101 years old and she lives up here with the rest of the family. Her grandmother and grandfather bought this land here, before that the family lived just a little further up in the mountains. I'm what I guess you call a mountain man. I'm an old ginseng hunter. I've made my living digging herbs and shrubs to sell from these mountains and doing landscape work for the folks around here. I've been singing and blowing a harp since I was a boy. Music is my enjoyment.

In his home, Society Hill, Alabama, 1996 *Duffy*

Robert Thomas

I used to perform with Uncle Albert Macon. He was my friend, he taught me to play behind him when I was a young boy. We used to play for house parties, fish fries, all sorts of gatherings. We even traveled to Europe to perform. He died and it has never been the same since. I really do miss my old partner.

ROBERT THOMAS, born in 1920, in Society Hill, Alabama, plays a type of music he calls "boogie and blues," which he learned from his best friend Albert Macon. For forty years the two played music together at fish fries, parties, and festivals in the greater Auburn and Tuskegee, Alabama, and Columbus, Georgia, areas. They also received national and international attention, playing at the Knoxville World's Fair and the American Blues Festival in the Netherlands and the WDR Blues Festival in Bonn, Germany. Macon and Thomas recorded *Blues and Boogie from Alabama,* an album on the Dutch Swingmaster label, and are also featured on the recording *In Celebration of a Legacy: Traditional Music of the Chattahoochee River Valley,* produced by the Columbus Museum of Art. They performed old-time, country blues tunes, such as "John Henry" and "Staggerlee," in a rousing style intended for dancing until Albert Macon's death in the nineties. Robert still plays guitar but remains deeply mournful of the loss of his best friend and musical partner.

Robert Thomas Field Notes
2/24/1995

MY HUSBAND TIM AND I ARE BACK ON THE ROAD BY 3:00 P.M. We decide we will check in on the other guys in the area on the rebound, and beeline for Alabama. A pit stop for dinner, groceries, and bottled water is mandatory before heading to Robert Thomas's place in the backwoods—no electricity, no telephone, and no running water. I love this place! The smoke hangs thick over the scattered patches of black-water swamp. As we pull in, the last rays of the late winter's sun still grip the bare clapboard walls of Robert Thomas's birth-place, a windowless, one-room sharecropper's shack. There is no one home but a one-eyed blue-tick hound. The light is luscious and Tim shoots some film. We prepare the van and ourselves for the coming night and head down to George Daniel's place a few miles away to see if he knows where Robert is. George is a player himself and he may just have the rank-est electric sound in the South. His amp is a living hell, but he is a great singer and har-monica player when we can get him to unplug. Sure enough, George leads us over to Robert's new girlfriend's house. Directions from Columbus, Georgia—head out on 80 West to Society Hill just before the turn off to Robert's house (Road 79 on left), take a right onto Road 91, then a quick right onto a dirt road, go two to three miles until you hit 80 again,

continue across and go another one and one-half to two miles, then take a right go another one-half to two miles and veer to the right at the fork in front of the white house. Go another mile or so. Claudia's house is a brick house on the right, with a wire fence in front—just after the house with the crazy painted tire fence in front.

WE SET UP AND ROLL SOME TAPE, but the guys aren't focused and we're not sure if we're getting any usable cuts. 'Round midnight we knock off and go back to Robert's place to crash. It's gotten very cold since the sun went down. Robert builds a fire and invites us to warm ourselves before turning in. The fire throws a dim flickering light over the bare, boarded walls. Patched with cardboard cartons and embellished with wildlife sketches torn from the pages of magazines, our host explains the house is about 100 years old and white people used to live here. It is crowded inside with what remains. Robert proudly shows us his new boots in the corner. They look out of place. Little new has ever come into these walls, nothing has ever left. Warm and tired we creep back to the van and nod off.

BY 6:00 A.M. ROBERT IS CHOPPING WOOD for the morning fire—rather loudly and close to the van on purpose. It's time to get going. The frost is thick on the windows and Tim and I are stiff from getting cold in the night. We go with Robert to deliver a load of wood. He makes arrangements to use a friend's "club" to record in. He has an errand to run and instructs us to go set up. He promises to follow in a few minutes. We are directed down twisting dirt roads, carved deep into the sandy earth by the rains of many winters. The edges are soft and wet; I imagine them to be quicksand. The van is wide and I am nervous. It is not quite spring in Alabama and the woods are still dense. Vines are stripped but the naked brush is thick enough to tangle a hiker's ankles. It must be magical in June when the jungle is in bloom. Humble and homemade houses are sparsely scattered along our route. There are also what appear to be campsites alongside the road. A fire pit, some old folding chairs, a ragged sofa, and a trash pile evidence some sort of domicile but were the inhabitants homeless or vacationing? Landowners or squatters? I don't ask— I'm afraid of embarrassing Robert or myself.

PEOPLE BUILD AND DECORATE TO THEIR OWN TASTES HERE and utilize what is readily available. A long fence made of used tires half-buried and brightly painted frames a lawn and walkway. I note it in my files; it will serve as a good landmark on future trips. What a lot of heavy work it must have been to make. I think of the picture-pretty New England towns I was surrounded by growing up and how the town historical (hysterical) council would condemn such a fence, socially ostracizing its creator for time immemorial. Folks here would balk at the idea of someone else imposing an aesthetic on them. They make no distinction between "folk art" and "fine art"; the need to qualify and

label is absent altogether. I was raised to qualify, note that when I mentioned today's recording site above I put the word *club* in quotes—implying that this space was not a real club—but some sort of facsimile. To Robert and the locals a place where people meet to hear music, dance, and buy drinks is a nightclub. Was I to hear this description I would agree, but I'm here now. The walls are bare cinder blocks, the floor cold cement, a much too tall plywood bar and large refrigerator, gray folding chairs and long tables of the sort used in church basements. It's damp and chilly. Robert's friend has kindly built a fire in a small potbelly stove. He's got to use small chunks of wood as the stove was made for coal. We are not introduced and he remains silent except for the scraping of the trowel he uses to tend the fire. Another man Robert introduces as his girlfriend's brother has come to observe the session. They proudly reminisce that he was also a guitar player at one time, but he hung it up years ago. He tries to fret a guitar but his nails are too long.

ROBERT BEGINS TO PLAY. He plays the blues simply with no tricks but with great joy. His bold smile is for everyone, his speech is uncomplicated and void of cliché and cynicism; he is a naturally charming man who seems much younger than his sixty-five years.

ROBERT DOESN'T WRITE HIS OWN SONGS but plays blues standards or the music of his deceased partner, Albert Macon. But his voice is his own and his simple guitar style brings one back to the early decades of the twentieth century. He lays down several tunes back to back. He's fine but most takes are ruined. The girlfriend's brother keeps opening his mouth in an effort to make small talk with the silent fire keeper. Finally, the blabbermouth leaves. The subsequent cuts are ruined by the fire-render banging around in the stove. Tim and I trade glances and wonder if he knows the sound is damaging. It's his club and he's gone to such effort to keep us warm in it, we don't have the heart to say anything. Before we leave I feel compelled to give the guy twenty bucks.

BY NOON OR ONE O'CLOCK WE PACK IT UP and say our good-byes to Robert. We head north to Opelika, hoping to find Eddie Eiland, a slide guitar player we missed on our last trip. The journey is only twenty-five to thirty miles, but by the time we get there we both feel lousy. Sleeping in the van last night, the cold and damp really got to our bones. We concede to being the wimpy, hothouse flowers we were raised to be, check in to the Super 8 and run a hot bath. Tim tries to ring up Eddie but he isn't in. Nap time. We finally catch Eddie at home in the early evening but he says he can't see us tonight or tomorrow. We manage to find a half-decent fish house for dinner and call it a day.

—DENISE DUFFY

With Macavine Hayes (*left*), Pinnacle, North Carolina, 1998 *Austin*

Haskel "Whistlin' Britches" Thompson

HASKEL THOMPSON was born in Winston-Salem, North Carolina, in 1932, and has lived there to this day. Captain Luke gave Haskel his nickname Whistlin' Britches years ago. He has an amazing spirit and exudes utter joy when he sings. He is the only fellow I have heard who can pop and click his tongue like a Bushman.

It is great being part of Music Maker and meeting different artists. I love it to the death. I love knowing that we are trying to help people. It is wonderful going out to entertain because we bring happiness, joy, and peace. I got children out here clicking and going on. When they see me they say, "Here comes the clicker." They try their best to do it. It makes me feel so good to be recognized. I want to sing it, I want to talk about it, I want to dance with it, I want to spread the news of our organization.

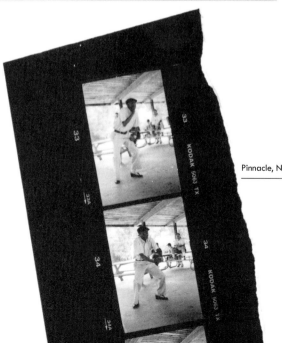

Pinnacle, North Carolina, 1998 *Duffy*

Chicago, 1999 *Duffy*

Eddie Tigner

EDDIE TIGNER was born on August 11, 1926, in Macon, Georgia. After his father died from mustard gas in World War I, his mother married a coal miner who moved the family to a mining camp in Kentucky. Eddie fondly remembers listening to bluegrass and country and western music as a child. When he was fourteen, the family moved to Atlanta, and Eddie started following his piano-playing mother to house parties, breakdowns, fish fries, and barbecues, where she was in demand as an entertainer.

Eddie didn't learn to play the piano himself, however, until he began his service in the army in 1945 after being taught by a friend, Edward Louis, at a base in Maryland. Eddie was in charge of booking entertainment at the special service hall each weekend, and often drove to Baltimore to pick up Bill Kenney (of the original Ink Spots) and his group to perform for the servicemen.

Returning to Atlanta after his discharge, Eddie joined the Musicians Union in 1947 and put together his first group, the Maroon Notes, in which he played vibes. They performed in vaudeville shows at theaters in Atlanta, and often toured through small towns as far as the West Coast of Florida. Eddie also played with legendary blues guitarist Elmore James during the early fifties, when James was living in Atlanta. They performed on weekends at the Lithonia Country Club, which featured all-black motorcycle and stock car races each Saturday.

In 1959, a version of the Ink Spots—one of several that traversed the country playing hotel lounges using the name of the original group—had a show in Atlanta and needed a pianist. Eddie joined the band and performed steadily as an Ink Spot until 1987.

These days, Eddie "feeds the children" at his job in an elementary school cafeteria, but he's also been playing in small clubs around Atlanta since 1991. Since connecting with the Music Maker Relief Foundation, he has appeared at major events including the Chicago Blues Festival and the Blues to Bop Festival in Lugano, Switzerland.

Samson, Alabama, 1993 *Küstner*

Perry Tillis

Blind from birth, **PERRY TILLIS** spent his youth in the country outside of the small town of Elba in southeast Alabama learning from older bluesmen. As a young man he traveled throughout the South performing on street corners. He met many musicians in his wanderings but Blind Willie Johnson, whose style Tillis's resembles, and Muddy Waters, who was just starting out in Clarksdale at the time, made a deep impression on him. "If you're a musician it's hard to escape dreamy-eyed women and strong liquor. When I saw what my drinkin' and good timin' was doing to my family. I decided to put a stop to it," Tillis reflected. "My sinful life just tore my family to pieces, and I hated to see that, 'cause I loved my kids. With God's help I made it." Perry became a preacher and stopped playing the blues but has a wonderful repertoire of deeply personal and traditional religious songs.

Barbeque at Othar's, Gravel Springs, Mississippi, 1991 *Küstner*

Othar Turner

My mama gave me a snare drum, that was a Christmas present. I played it so much I busted it. She bought me another and I busted that one too. Then I got me a fifty-gallon lard can—that still sittin' out there yonder.

Well into his nineties, fife and drum bandleader **OTHAR TURNER** is still actively "blowin' cane" with his family group, the Rising Star Fife and Drum Band, as he has since roughly 1923. His granddaughter Sharday has become an expert fife player and along with her brothers she will keep this ancient music alive for generations to come. Turner lives in Senatobia, Mississippi.

With granddaughter Sharday, Old Memphis, Alabama, 1999 *Duffy*

Ariton, Alabama, 2001 *Küstner*

J. W. Warren

Born in 1921, **J. W. WARREN** lives in Ozark, Alabama, and is a veteran of WWII. In his young days he dated Big Mamma Thornton when they were scuffling around together in juke joints down in Alabama. When I met him he told me that he had given up his music. I convinced him to record and was amazed by J. W.'s original story songs and his guitar style in which he used his old jackknife as a slide.

I came up the hard way, I never had a break whatsoever. In other words, I never had a break in my life. I was born in the wrong part of the world and then again I didn't go any place better, you know what I mean? I been around the States and overseas but it seems like I can make it better here than any place else. My daddy gave me a good raising and I know how to treat people, how to be respectful to folks, I like that. But I had too much trouble in my life. I didn't do anything with the kind of talent I had because I didn't have that much education. I had to walk six miles to school and then six miles back. When the creek got up I couldn't get there at all! When you got a bad break like I had, you doubt yourself. You know it's rough, man.

Ozark, Alabama, 1996 *Duffy*

Cotton Club, Atlanta, 1998 *Austin*

Beverly "Guitar" Watkins

from "Miz Dr. Feelgood"

You don't need no shots,
You don't need no pills
Let my guitar cure all your ills.

They call me Miz Dr. Feelgood
I said hey, hey, hey
Well it's my time now, I'm going to rock your blues away.

Winston Blues Revival
Neighborhood Theater | Charlotte, North Carolina
February 25, 1999

There's nothing on the stage and then a haze overtakes the place and then **BEVERLY "GUITAR" WATKINS** comes out of nowhere. Out of nowhere at all. And she's led by a red Fender Mustang guitar, and she's still hanging on to fifty-nine-years-old and she leaps and points the guitar neck and shouts and struts and poses. Out of nowhere. Then she runs and drops to her knees and plays the solo to "Rock Me Baby." And Macavine Hayes, who'd already got up and sung about "I got a woman way over town she's good to me," stands in the middle of the aisle and claps and dances and wears a laminated pass on a lanyard around his neck that reads "All Access—Ain't No Place I Can't Go."

Beverly plays a couple more songs and, no joke, gets a standing ovation after each song. Out of nowhere. And it's business as usual, she'll admit later on. Then she all of a sudden turns her back. Turns her back to the same crowd that had never heard of her before tonight but that is now screaming her name over and over again like she'd forget it if they didn't. And then, get

this, she lifts that red guitar up and over her head and then down. She sets it behind her head. Sets it behind her head and plays it like it's a normal thing for a fifty-nine-year-old woman to do on a Thursday night in Charlotte. Out of nowhere, she plays it behind her head.

And then there's just bedlam.

Turns out she's from somewhere. Turns out she's from Atlanta; born there April 6, 1939. Turns out she played guitar on records that made John Lennon want to be John Lennon.

"Back then I didn't do nothing but looked pretty and played rhythm," Watkins says. She's talking about her days as a teenage guitarist for the legendary Piano Red. She's talking about wearing a nurse's uniform for the cover photo shoot for his album that featured "Dr. Feelgood." (She agreed to the uniform, but drew the line at wearing the nurse's shoes.) She's talking about the history of rock and roll, of blues, of rhythm and blues.

And that's not the beginning of it. The beginning was gospel music. Shortly after was Roy Acuff singing "Great Speckle Bird" through a transistor radio speaker. And then there was her granddaddy, Luke Hayes, playing the banjo on the front porch. And then there was the Hayes Sisters.

"That was my aunts," Watkins explains. "They sang a lot. And they used to buy Sister Rosetta Tharpe 45's and bring them down for Christmas to where I called home. That was in the country in Commerce, Georgia. I guess there was something about Sister Rosetta. There was something about this woman playing the guitar. I guess it just amused me. It was surprising."

It was Commerce to Atlanta, then it was English Avenue Elementary School to Billy West Stone and the Downbeats combo. That was in about 1958. For Billy West Stone's group, she played rhythm and bass.

"Every song we did, I would tune my low E-string down to whatever song we were going to do," she says. "If we were doing the song in F, I would tune that string to F. It was hard for me, 'cause I didn't start knowing about music until I started getting around to the eighth grade. Then after I started getting into high school, then I kindly went to music classes, started going to libraries, reading about different musicians and guitar players."

Her high school band teacher used to help her out. She played trumpet in his marching band, but before long he ordered a guitar for her to play. He showed her how to tune the guitar correctly and how to play the scales.

"See, during that time I was smart," she says. "I made all A's in music. I began to update myself on guitar, playing with Mr. Lloyd Terry at Archer High School in Atlanta, Georgia. We had a good band. Gladys Knight went to our school and she was the majorette. Anyway, I rocked on, rocked on, kept going."

Billy West's was mostly a jazz group. "Misty," "Summertime," and such as that. Once they played the Yamaha Club on Simpson Avenue and Piano Red's drummer, Bobby Tuggle, was there to listen. He liked what he heard, took Beverly to meet Piano Red, and they up and formed the Meter Tones. Watkins remembers riding in Red's blue 1958 Ford to club gigs in Monroe and Carrollton and Marietta.

And that was all right, but it got better when bass man Tommy Legon joined up.

"He turned everything around," Watkins says. "He was so far advanced into music. He would get myself and [lead guitarist] Curtis Smith, buy us a book, and show us how to play chords without using the capo across our strings. One time we played at Georgia Tech, picked up the guitars and found out he'd hid those capos. Tommy wasn't with the band too long, but there was quite a lot of learning going on with him."

After a few years, the Meter Tones gave way to the first version of Dr. Feelgood and the Interns, which gave later way to the second incarnation. That one had Roy Lee Johnson, Howard Hobbs, Smith, and Tuggle.

Winston Blues Revival napkin, Austin, Texas, 1999 *Duffy*

"We rehearsed sometimes five days a week," Watkins says. "Mr. Red wanted his band on time and together. If we rehearsed and didn't get but one tune that day, that was progress. If you didn't play a chord right, we stayed there all day. He said, 'I want the band tight and I want it played right.'"

They played a lot of colleges. They played the University of Georgia and Yale. They played Mississippi in segregation days and they slept in a station wagon because they couldn't get a motel room. They made records that went all over the world, all the way to Liverpool, England, and into the hands of the Beatles who thought "Dr. Feelgood" and "Right String but the Wrong Yo-Yo" came out of nowhere. And the Interns rocked on, rocked on, kept going. And when they got out of the station wagon they rehearsed.

Watkins next joined up with original Ink Spot Eddie Tigner. That gig became less steady seven months later, when Tigner suffered a minor stroke and had to come off the road.

"I believe I worked at every car wash in Atlanta after that," Watkins says. "And I cleaned houses and offices, and I went out to play guitar on weekends when Mr. Tigner would have a show."

Then there was a succession of bands. There was Joseph Smith and the Fendales. There was Leroy Redding and the Houserockers. There was an all-woman band that played regularly at an Atlanta lesbian bar called the Other Side. Sometimes she played in nightclubs, sometimes churches, sometimes solo, sometimes on the streets, sometimes in the food court at the Underground Atlanta shopping mall.

Along the way, she started singing and playing lead guitar. "People are surprised when a black woman can play the guitar like a man. Some people say, 'I've got to hear this, 'cause I don't believe she can do it.' I say, 'Just wait until showtime comes.' Then when I go on and come off, they say—excuse the expression—'Damn, I ain't never seen nothin' like you.'

"I kept on, understand."

—PETER COOPER

With Cootie Stark (*right*), and Sammy Blue (*left*), Northside Tavern, Atlanta, 1997 *Austin*

On a throne by Sam McMillan,
Pinnacle, North Carolina, 1999 *Austin*

Ernie Williams

from "Just Another Day"

You broke my heart when you went away
I go through these moments but it's just another day
Some women have faces that look like you
No woman could ever take your place
Oh I miss loving you

ERNIE WILLIAMS spent his youth in the thirties picking tobacco by day and playing the blues at night in his shack on a Virginia plantation. In the forties he joined the bluesmen in his community playing at fish fries in Halifax County. At the age of nineteen he took one year to save nine dollars to buy a one-way ticket to Harlem. There he played amateur nights at the Apollo and juke joints throughout the city. By the seventies he had relocated to Albany, New York, where he has performed regularly to this day. In his seventies, Ernie is still gigging regularly and is a beloved figure in his adopted hometown.

Poulan, Georgia, 1996 *Duffy*

Jimmie Lee Williams

When you had a party they stayed up till the break of day. They stayed as long as that guitar stayed there, they wouldn't go. Oh boy, we had a good time. Nobody playing but me and my baby brother. I wish he was here now. Boy, I wish we could play together again.

JIMMIE LEE WILLIAMS (1925–1999) was born in Worth County, Georgia, where he has lived and farmed all his life. "People used to be a lot more healthy when they was plowing with mules than now with tractors. You just sitting there on that tractor all day and if you know how to drive one you just sit up there and go to sleep," Williams says. "But with that mule you got to be stepping behind him and I always had a fast mule and I had to go to stay up with him. I plowed with mules ever since I was seven years old. I loved it."

from "Hoot Your Belly"

Hoot your belly, give your backbone ease
Baby around here, love just who you please.

Love that woman, just can't call her name
Married woman, but I love her just the same.

I'm going, I'm going, crying won't make me stay
The more you cry, the further you drive me away.

Kathleen, Georgia, 1996 *Duffy*

John Lee Zeigler

"Zeigler's music is the last footprint of the African music before it took the next step into Southern music. His song 'Going Away' is a very deep and ancient piece of music."

—TAJ MAHAL

Born in 1929 in Kathleen, Georgia, **JOHN LEE ZEIGLER** plays the guitar left-handed, with the strings upside down, striking the bass strings with his index finger and the treble strings with his thumb. John is unique, the most pure Georgia blues artist performing today.

Gray, Georgia, 2000

AFTERWORD

The founding of the Music Maker Relief Foundation was purely a heartfelt reaction to the poverty and lack of recognition faced by Guitar Gabriel and the blues artists in and around Winston-Salem, North Carolina. In the early days there was no long-term plan for the organization, it was simply an immediate way to provide food and medicine to a small group of deserving artists. When MMRF arranged for Guitar Gabriel and Willa Mae Buckner to perform at Carnegie Hall in 1994, it was our most glorious achievement. To Gabe and Willa it signified reaching a level of respect they had aspired to for over fifty years. It was a great day.

Those days passed and so did Gabe and Willa. During the early years our primary focus was on record company and touring contracts. These business arrangements were all well and good for the artists that we could get gigs for, but there were always more artists than available deals. As the years passed the numbers of artists began to grow. It then became clear to us that for MMRF to continue to prosper and serve its constituents we needed to dedicate more of our time to its development.

We began helping dozens of artists with their dreams of making a career. Cootie Stark emerged and explained to us his lifelong desire to be recognized for his music. He was tired of playing street corners and the local pizza joint for fifty dollars. Since our meeting he has toured Europe over a dozen times, played more than thirty-six major venues across the

U.S., and is respected as a great Piedmont bluesman. Cootie's life has improved materially but, more importantly, he is proud of his accomplishments, has dozens of new friends, and sees his future as full of opportunity. This sort of transformation is what we are working for.

The people in this book are artists that we recognize as important talents. We have helped a great deal of them but many have not yet received the benefit of all of our programs. Our resources must grow to make a difference for these folks. To this end we have seriously dedicated our lives to building the foundation.

We began working from an old utility building and now have our headquarters in Hillsborough, North Carolina. My family lives in a log house at the end of a winding road, nestled up to a five-hundred-acre state park. I converted an old woodshop on the property into our studio and offices and built a guest cottage where artists can reside when they come to visit.

The walls of this small compound are hung with the many photographs, posters, and other artifacts from years well spent with these musicians. My wife Denise and I wake up each morning and go to work to keep the mission alive. John Ferguson lives down the road and when artists visit, they all want to go hang with him and listen to his guitar. When Taj Mahal comes and visits with us, I arrange for different artists to come by each day and rehearse their music with this Grammy-winning artist.

In our small way we are giving these artists the respect that they desire and deserve. Today there is a booming interest in roots music but there never seems to be any new, authentic roots performers being celebrated. Our hope is that this book shows fans the number of living talents continuing these traditions among us.

DISCOGRAPHY of Music Maker Recordings

THE BLUES WAS A TEXTBOOK, and the hero-filled pages—rife with stories of Lightnin' Hopkins, Robert Johnson, Muddy Waters, and the whole lot of them—had yellowed. The prime players had been identified, classified, and set on an accepted timeline. It was all neat and clean.

Upcountry Mississippi's still-thriving juke joints served notice that the textbook was missing some vital information but, as little as a decade ago, no one thought that a loosely affiliated, stylistically diverse collection of unheralded musicians from the Carolinas, Georgia, Alabama, and West Virginia would call into question the accuracy of the accepted American roots music story.

Because, you see, nobody had heard Cootie Stark sing "Jigroo," a Piedmont blues song that is one part unmitigated joy and one part deep mystery. Stark's voice now blasts from stereo speakers like the aural equivalent of some long-rumored playground basketball legend suddenly sprung to life, battling Michael Jordan on an NBA arena's gleaming hardwood.

Where Cootie comes from, the Jordans of Piedmont blues are Reverend Gary Davis, Pink Anderson, and Baby Tate. Stark's *Sugar Man*, released as part of the Music Maker series of albums, puts him on the all-star team, securing a historical place for an artist who evaded discovery during the folk boom of the 1960s and 1970s and musicologist Samuel Charters' trips to South Carolina. Neither throngs of Woodstockers and Newporters nor Pete Seeger

and Charters found all the good stuff. Cootie Stark sat blind and alone, playing the streets of Asheville, Spartanburg, Columbia, and Greenville.

Sugar Man doesn't merely proclaim "Cootie Stark was here." It is evidence that Stark was, and is, an idiosyncratic, tremendously talented musician. It's a sonic monument, and a reality check that immediately calls into question the textbook pages dedicated to Piedmont blues.

And, as a part of the Music Maker recordings, it is not alone. Now more than twenty albums strong, the Music Maker series is a most important addition to the blues canon. It sheds light in dark rooms, asks new questions, and offers musicologists and fans quite a lesson in the truth of the old axiom "the more I learn, the less I know."

Here is Captain Luke, rumbling low and wise enough to make Barry White sound pre-adolescent. Here is Cool John Ferguson, laying down tracks that led Grammy-winner Taj Mahal to proclaim him one of the world's finest guitarists. Here is grandfatherly Carl Rutherford's devastating take on "The Old Rugged Cross," and Macavine Hayes' gutbucket growl on "Let's Talk It Over," and Willa Mae Buckner's ribald "Peter Rumpkin." Here is Preston Fulp's marrow-deep take on "Careless Love."

Here is Beverly "Guitar" Watkins, previously heard from as one of Dr. Feelgood's Interns, decreeing herself "Back in Business." Here are subtler but no less wondrous musical flights from Etta Baker, Precious Bryant, and Samuel Turner Stevens. Here is astounding harmonica work from Abe Reid, Neal Pattman, and the great Jerry "Boogie" McCain.

It's a remarkable catalogue, particularly given the fact that the Music Maker organization spends more time aiding musicians in daily subsistence than putting out records. In the hierarchy of needs, food and clothing are more essential than the production of compact discs. But in the grand scheme, these discs are vital.

There's a lot of talk these days in non-profit circles about "outcome-based" analysis. The United Way, for example, now refuses funding to organizations that cannot show quantifiable results and offer hard proof that good intentions are providing positive, measurable outcomes.

Here, then, are the outcomes. They are confirmation that Music Maker caters to unjustly overlooked, should-be musical heroes. They are inspirational documentation of the blues' ever-evolving life. They are the latest indication that the blues tale is an unsolved riddle, not a story. They are paper-shredders to the textbook, and they are prayers offered in the hope that the Music Maker Relief Foundation is not merely a beautiful aberration but a genuine revival.

And, more to the point, where the hell else are you going to hear this stuff?

—PETER COOPER

Little Pink Anderson
Carolina Bluesman
MMCD 24

Etta Baker
Railroad Bill
91006-2

Essie Mae Brooks
Rain in Your Life
MMCD 15

Captain Luke and
    Cool John
Outsider Lounge Music
CL100

Cool John Ferguson
Cool John Ferguson
MMCD 18

Cora Mae Bryant
Born with the Blues
MMCD22

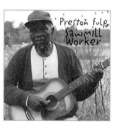

Preston Fulp
Sawmill Worker
MMCD 20

Guitar Gabriel
Volume 1
MMCD0494

Guitar Gabriel
Deep in the South
91001-2

George Higgs
Tarboro Blues
MMCD 19

Algia Mae Hinton
Honey Babe
91005-2

John Dee Holeman
Bull Durham Blues
91004-2

Jerry "Boogie" McCain
This Stuff Just Kills Me
90005-2

Jerry "Boogie" McCain
Unplugged
MMCD 21

Neal Pattman
Prison Blues
MMKCD 703
featuring Taj Mahal and Lee Konitz

Carl Rutherford
Turn Off the Fear
MMCD 17

Cootie Stark
Sugar Man
MMCD 8
featuring Taj Mahal and Lee Konitz

Eddie Tigner
Route 66
MMCD 16

Beverly "Guitar" Watkins
Back in Business
91007-2

Lightnin' Wells
Ragged but Right
MMCD 26

Music Maker Relief Foundation
4052 Summer Lane
Hillsborough, NC 27278
(919) 643.2456 (telephone) / (919) 643.2597 (fax)
www.musicmaker.org / mmrf1@aol.com

Compilations

Songs from the Roots of America II
MMCD 28

This compilation of true gems from Timothy Duffy's field recording trips feature artists profiled in this book but not found on its accompanying CD. Most of the tracks have never been issued.

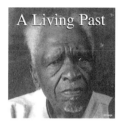

A Living Past
MMCD 9401

The first album in the Music Maker series, a sampler of the traditional blues scene in North Carolina, has been heralded by reviewers throughout the world as a classic recording. The disc leads off with Guitar Gabriel's "Came So Far" and includes seventeen tracks by eight artists.

Blues Came to Georgia
MMCD23

Georgians are among the greatest contributors to blues, the roots of all modern popular music. This album, with songs by thirteen artists, celebrates Georgia's deep contribution to our musical universe.

Came So Far
MMCD 1294

This album of eighteen selections by twelve astonishing blues and gospel artists (many never before recorded) was made in the field, in old trailers, kitchens, living rooms, and nursing homes. With all songs recorded in a single take, these heartfelt performances will make you laugh, cry, and shout as only the real blues can.

Expressin' the Blues
MMKCD 701

This album features twenty-one of the most talented and unsung heroes of the blues. With contributions from the likes of Captain Luke, Big Boy Henry, Samuel Turner Stevens, Cootie Stark, and Guitar Gabriel, *Expressin' the Blues* is a collection of some of the most emotional, gut-level music available on disc, the feelings intensified by the immediacy of the recordings.

sol
volume: blue
MMCD25

From Tim Duffy's archive of field recordings, sol creates an audio palette which takes the listener on an odyssey through the blues and gospel at their most real and rooted level.

CONTRIBUTORS

MARK AUSTIN was born in High Point, North Carolina, in 1952. He began working as a photographer at age seventeen. At twenty-five he went to sea, taking along his Leica and documenting the lives of commercial fisherman of the East Coast and Alaska. Austin's photographs of blues musicians have appeared in *Bikini, Esquire, Living Blues,* and *Rolling Stone.*

PETER COOPER lives in Nashville and has written about music for *The Oxford American, Creative Loafing, The* (Nashville) *Tennessean,* and the *Spartanburg* (S.C.) *Herald-Journal.* He is the author of *Hub City Music Makers: One Southern Town's Popular Music Legacy.*

After her graduation from Hampshire College, **DENISE DUFFY** and husband Tim lived in Mombasa, Kenya, eventually settling in North Carolina. In 1994, Denise embraced the Music Maker mission and left her corporate job to build the business structure of the foundation. She continues this work as MMRF's administrative director.

TIMOTHY DUFFY is president of the Music Maker Relief Foundation. His photographs have been exhibited at the Georgia Music Hall of Fame. He is a recipient of the National Guitars Lifetime Achievement Award and was named Producer of the Year by *Living Blues* magazine in 1999.

KEVIN HOPPE is a professional photographer who was a great fan of Guitar Gabriel.

AXEL KÜSTNER befriended blues legend Big Joe Williams who was on a European tour in 1972. Küstner made his first trip to the American South in 1978 to visit Williams and began his blues odyssey. With friend Ziggy Christman he produced the seminal *Living Country Blues USA* (1980), a series of field recordings made in an era in which little such work was done. Since being introduced to MMRF in 1991, Küstner has been an invaluable resource in conducting field research. He lives in Bad Gandersheim, Germany.

Two-time Grammy Award-winning bluesman **TAJ MAHAL** has been a major recording artist since his debut album in 1967. His career has included acting in television and movies; scoring for television, plays, and movies; and recording children's records. Much of his early work in the seventies set the groundwork for the present-day world music scene. Highlights of his career are collected in *In Progress & In Motion: 1965–1998* and *The Best of Taj Mahal.*

Playwright and director **TOBIAS MUNTHE** graduated from Oxford University with a degree in literature. He is lead vocalist and saxophonist for the Cambridge, England-based Loose Booty funk and blues band.

DAVID NELSON, former editor of *Living Blues,* writes about music for a number of publications. With Bill Ferris, he co-hosted Public Radio in Mississippi's *Highway 61* weekly blues show for nearly a decade. He lives in Snow Camp, North Carolina.

MIKE "LIGHTNIN'" WELLS of Farmville, North Carolina, is a performer of Southern music. An avid record collector and writer, he serves on the board of the Music Maker Relief Foundation.

WESLEY WILKES is a poet and writer who has been a supporter of the foundation for many years. He was a dear friend of Guitar Gabriel.

MUSIC CREDITS

Songs from the Roots of America I

Produced and recorded by Timothy Duffy
Mastered by Hansel Creech
Artistic consultant: Taj Mahal

1 | **John Dee Holeman and Taj Mahal**
Mistreated Blues
(J. D. Holeman, Lucky Guitar Music, ASCAP)
John Dee Holeman: vocals and guitar; Taj Mahal: piano

2 | **Captain Luke and Cool John**
Chokin' Kind
(Howard Harlan, Sony/Sony ATV Songs LLC, BMI)
Captain Luke: vocals; Cool John: guitars, bass, high hat; mixed by Hansel Creech

3 | **Neal Pattman and Taj Mahal**
Shortnin' Bread
(Trad. arr. by N. Pattman, Lucky Guitar Music, ASCAP)
Neal Pattman: vocals and harp; Taj Mahal: banjo

4 | **Guitar Gabriel and Lucille Lindsey**
Do You Know What It Means to Have a Friend?
(G. Gabriel, Lucky Guitar Music ASCAP)
Guitar Gabriel: vocals and guitar; Lucille Lindsey: vocals

5 | **Cootie Stark**
Jigroo
(C. Stark, Lucky Guitar Music, ASCAP)
Cootie Stark: vocals, guitar; Brothers in the Kitchen: Timothy Duffy, guitar; Ardie Dean, drums; Michael Parrish, piano; Abraham Reid, harp; Mark Tortenson, upright bass

6 | **Willa Mae Buckner**
Peter Rumpkin
(Trad. arr. by W. Buckner)
Willa Mae Buckner: vocals; Tim Duffy: guitar; Michael Parrish: piano

7 | **Algia Mae Hinton**
When You Kill a Chicken, Save Me the Head
(A. Hinton, Lucky Guitar Music ASCAP)
Algia Mae Hinton: vocals and twelve-string guitar

8 | **Carl Rutherford**
Turn Off the Fear
(C. Rutherford, Lucky Guitar Music, ASCAP)
Carl Rutherford: vocals, guitar, dobro; Cool John Ferguson: electric guitar; Jim O'Keefe: bass, back-up vocals

9 | **Beverly "Guitar" Watkins**
Miz Dr. Feelgood
(B. Watkins, Brand New Music Ltd, Admin. Bug Music Ltd.)
Beverly Watkins: vocals, guitar; Carl Sonny Leyland: piano; Danny "Mudcat" Dudeck: guitar; Jon Schwenke: bass; Chris Uhler: congas/percussion; Jason Reichert: drums; Mike Vernon: producer, recorded at Audio Arts, Smyrna, Georgia

10 | **Jerry "Boogie" McCain**
Where You Been?
(J. McCain, McBlues Music BMI)
Jerry McCain: vocals, harp; Carl Sonny Leland; Anson Funderburgh: guitar; Jimmie Vaughn: guitar; Dave Smith: bass; Steve Potts: drums; Mike Vernon: percussion and producer; recorded at Ardent Studios, Memphis, Tennessee

11 | **Essie Mae Brooks**
Rain in Your Life
(E.Brooks, Lucky Guitar Music, ASCAP)
Essie Mae Brooks: vocals

12 | **Etta Baker**
Carolina Breakdown
(E. Baker, Lucky Guitar Music, ASCAP)
Etta Baker: guitar

13 | **Big Boy Henry**
Old Bill
(R. Henry, Lucky Guitar Music, ASCAP)
Big Boy Henry: vocals; Tim Duffy and Michael Parrish: guitars

14 | **Samuel Turner Stevens**
Railroadin' and Gamblin'
(Traditional)
Samuel Turner Stevens: vocals, fretless banjo

15 | **John Lee Zeigler**
Goin' Away
(J. L. Zeigler, Lucky Guitar Music, ASCAP)
John Lee Zeigler: vocals, guitar

16 | **Macavine Hayes**
Let's Talk It Over
(Traditional)
Macavine Hayes: vocals; Tim Duffy: guitar; Michael Parrish: piano

17 | **Eddie Tigner**
C. C. Rider
(Traditional)
Eddie Tigner: vocals, piano, organ; Doug "Little Brother" Jones: guitar; Steve Hawkins: drums; John Weyland: bass; Larry Bowie: percussion; Donnie McCormick, Chris Light, and Larry Bowie: background vocals; Eddie Tigner: producer; recorded by Chris Light and Larry Bowie at Bellingreth Studios, Atlanta

18 | **Cora Mae Bryant**
Cold and Rainy Day
(Curley Weaver)
Cora Mae Bryant: vocals; Joshua Jacobson: guitar

19 | **George Higgs**
Greasy Greens
(Traditional)
George Higgs: vocals, harp

20 | **Cool John Ferguson**
Strollin' on the Waterfront
(J. Ferguson, Lucky Guitar Music, ASCAP)
Cool John Ferguson: vocals, guitar, sol: bass; Janet Daniels: drums

21 | **Precious Bryant**
Fever
(E. Cooley, J. Davenport, Fort Knox Music Inc., BMI)
Precious Bryant: vocals, guitar

22 | **sol**
Black Mattie
(sol, Lucky Guitar Music ASCAP)
Guitar Gabriel's vocals, Cool John Ferguson's lead and rhythm guitar, and Robert "Wolfman" Belfour's *Black Mattie*; sol: bass; sol: producer; field recordings by Timothy Duffy

Bonus | **Crickets**
Crickets of Pinnacle, North Carolina

Joe Lee Cole, Clarksdale, Mississippi, 2001 *Duffy*

ACKNOWLEDGMENTS

I AM ETERNALLY GRATEFUL TO MY FATHER AND MOTHER ALLEN AND LUCY DUFFY who nurtured my interest in the arts. My brothers Paul, Daniel, and Sam have all helped me along the way by traveling, performing, and helping me document these artists.

My entrée into the blues culture of the American South would not have been possible without the friendship of James "Guitar Slim" Stephens, Guitar Gabriel and his wife Dorothy, Willa Mae Buckner, Captain Luke, Macavine Hayes, Preston Fulp, and Mr. Q. These artists were patient and generous in teaching me the communication skills needed to travel in their world.

In my professional life I am deeply indebted to Bill Krasilovsky who has been our mentor and lawyer since 1989. Many thanks to Mark Levinson for putting us firmly on this path and to B. B. King and Norman Matthews for their generous spirits. Taj Mahal has been my counsel and has shown tremendous respect to these artists and the foundation. Bill Lucado deserves many thanks for his giant heart towards the musicians. I wish to thank Joe Michalek and R.J. Reynolds for launching the Winston Blues Campaign.

I am grateful to those individuals who help this cause with their hearts but who wish to remain anonymous.

My gratitude to all the photographers and writers who have given freely to this book and these artists.

I wish to acknowledge the work of folklorists Peter B. Lowrey, George Mitchell, Glenn Hinson, and Bruce Bastin whose trails I followed.

A special thanks to all the musicians who have recorded and performed with Music Maker artists over the years, especially Cool John Ferguson who makes us all sound better.

A note of appreciation must go to D'Addario for donating guitar strings to MMRF artists.

Thanks to *The Oxford American, Living Blues Magazine,* Kay Hill, Kathryn and Mudcat, Kim Cattrall, Nora Milner, the Jones family, Pete Townshend, Steve Riggio, Norman Hewitt, Lisa Love, Dave McGrew, Larry Shores, Eric Clapton, B. B. King, Nathaniel, Rick, Bonnie Raitt, Ardie Dean, John and Hansel Creech, Dennis Baird, Rachel Shabott, Abe Reid, Don Saverese, Bill Puckett, Tim Clarke, Fred and Kim Tamalonis, Katharine Walton, Larry and Linda Garrett, Deborah Misch, David and Peggy Moore, John Price, Brad Bennett, Kay Hill, Spike Barkin, Lightnin' Wells, the Georgia Music Hall of Fame, Lewis Goldstein, Michael Parrish, Peter and Dede DeVries, David Burcham, Gaile Welker, and Erica Darling, who have all have given their work and time to MMRF artists.

Most importantly, thanks must go to my wife Denise and our children Lucas and Lilla who join me in this life every day.

MUSIC MAKER
Relief Foundation

Contributions to the foundation through direct donations and purchasing of music not available in most book and record stores is available through the Music Maker Relief Foundation's website:

www.musicmaker.org

At this site you can become a Friend of Music Makers by signing up for a free subscription to their quarterly publication, *Music Maker Rag,* which features documentary photography, tour dates, artist profiles, and CD releases for artists assisted by the foundation. There is also information about their "Givin' It Back Record Club" which provides members with four CDs per year and other opportunities to support their work and enjoy stellar American roots music.

Music Maker Relief Foundation
919.643.2456

Music Maker Relief Foundation is a 501(c)3 tax exempt organization.
All donations are tax-deductible to the full extent allowed by law.